MAX LUCADO

LIFE LESSONS *from*

EZRA & NEHEMIAH

Lessons in Leadership

PREPARED BY THE LIVINGSTONE CORPORATION

THOMAS NELSON
Since 1798

Published in Nashville, Tennessee, by Thomas Nelson. Thomas Nelson is a registered trademark of HarperCollins Christian Publishing, Inc.

Produced with the assistance of the Livingstone Corporation (www.livingstonecorp.com).

All Scripture quotations, unless otherwise indicated, are taken from The Holy Bible, New International Version®, NIV®. Copyright © 1973, 1978, 1984, 2011 by Biblica, Inc.™ Used by permission. All rights reserved worldwide.

Scripture quotations marked MSG are taken from The Message. Copyright © 1993, 1994, 1995, 1996, 2000, 2001, 2002. Used by permission of NavPress Publishing Group.

Scripture quotations marked NKJV are taken from the New King James Version®. Copyright © 1982 by Thomas Nelson. Used by permission. All rights reserved.

Scripture quotations marked TLB are taken from The Living Bible. Copyright © 1971 by Tyndale House Foundation. Used by permission of Tyndale House Publishers Inc., Carol Stream, Illinois 60188. All rights reserved.

Material for the "Inspiration" sections taken from the following books:

And the Angels Were Silent. Copyright © 1987 by Max Lucado. Thomas Nelson, a registered trademark of HarperCollins Christian Publishing, Inc., Nashville, Tennessee.

The Applause of Heaven. Copyright © 1990 by Max Lucado. Thomas Nelson, a registered trademark of HarperCollins Christian Publishing, Inc., Nashville, Tennessee.

Because of Bethlehem. Copyright © 2016 by Max Lucado. Thomas Nelson, a registered trademark of HarperCollins Christian Publishing, Inc., Nashville, Tennessee.

Fearless. Copyright © 2009 by Max Lucado. Thomas Nelson, a registered trademark of HarperCollins Christian Publishing, Inc., Nashville, Tennessee.

Glory Days. Copyright © 2015 by Max Lucado. Thomas Nelson, a registered trademark of HarperCollins Christian Publishing, Inc., Nashville, Tennessee.

Great Day Every Day (previously published as *Every Day Deserves a Chance*). Copyright © 2007, 2012 by Max Lucado. Thomas Nelson, a registered trademark of HarperCollins Christian Publishing, Inc., Nashville, Tennessee.

Hand Me Another Brick. Copyright © 1990 by Charles Swindoll. Thomas Nelson, a registered trademark of HarperCollins Christian Publishing, Inc., Nashville, Tennessee.

Just Like Jesus. Copyright © 1998 by Max Lucado. Thomas Nelson, a registered trademark of HarperCollins Christian Publishing, Inc., Nashville, Tennessee.

Max on Life. Copyright © 2010 by Max Lucado. Thomas Nelson, a registered trademark of HarperCollins Christian Publishing, Inc., Nashville, Tennessee.

More to Your Story. Copyright © 2011, 2016 by Max Lucado. Thomas Nelson, a registered trademark of HarperCollins Christian Publishing, Inc., Nashville, Tennessee.

Shaped by God (previously published as *On the Anvil*). Copyright © 2001 by Max Lucado. Tyndale House Publishers, Carol Stream, Illinois.

Walking with Christ in the Details of Life. Copyright © 1992 by Patrick Morley. Thomas Nelson, a registered trademark of HarperCollins Christian Publishing, Inc., Nashville, Tennessee.

Thomas Nelson titles may be purchased in bulk for educational, business, fundraising, or sales promotional use. For information, please e-mail SpecialMarkets@ThomasNelson.com.

ISBN 978-0-310-08672-7

First Printing February 2019 / Printed in the United States of America

CONTENTS

HOW TO STUDY THE BIBLE

The Bible is a peculiar book. Words crafted in another language. Deeds done in a distant era. Events recorded in a far-off land. Counsel offered to a foreign people. It is a peculiar book.

It's surprising that anyone reads it. It's too old. Some of its writings date back 5,000 years. It's too bizarre. The book speaks of incredible floods, fires, earthquakes, and people with supernatural abilities. It's too radical. The Bible calls for undying devotion to a carpenter who called himself God's Son.

Logic says this book shouldn't survive. Too old, too bizarre, too radical.

The Bible has been banned, burned, scoffed, and ridiculed. Scholars have mocked it as foolish. Kings have branded it as illegal. A thousand times over the grave has been dug and the dirge has begun, but somehow the Bible never stays in the grave. Not only has it survived, but it has also thrived. It is the single most popular book in all of history. It has been the bestselling book in the world for years!

There is no way on earth to explain it. Which perhaps is the only explanation. For the Bible's durability is not found on *earth* but in *heaven*. The millions who have tested its claims and claimed its promises know there is but one answer: the Bible is God's book and God's voice.

As you read it, you would be wise to give some thought to two questions: *What is the purpose of the Bible?* and *How do I study the Bible?* Time spent reflecting on these two issues will greatly enhance your Bible study.

What is the purpose of the Bible?

Let the Bible itself answer that question: *"From infancy you have known the Holy Scriptures, which are able to make you wise for salvation through faith in Christ Jesus"* (2 Timothy 3:15).

The purpose of the Bible? Salvation. God's highest passion is to get his children home. His book, the Bible, describes his plan of salvation. The purpose of the Bible is to proclaim God's plan and passion to save his children.

This is the reason why this book has endured through the centuries. It dares to tackle the toughest questions about life: *Where do I go after I die? Is there a God? What do I do with my fears?* The Bible is the treasure map that leads to God's highest treasure—eternal life.

But how do you study the Bible? Countless copies of Scripture sit unread on bookshelves and nightstands simply because people don't know how to read it. What can you do to make the Bible real in your life?

The clearest answer is found in the words of Jesus: *"Ask and it will be given to you; seek and you will find; knock and the door will be opened to you"* (Matthew 7:7).

The first step in understanding the Bible is asking God to help you. You should read it prayerfully. If anyone understands God's Word, it is because of God and not the reader.

"The Advocate, the Holy Spirit, whom the Father will send in my name, will teach you all things and will remind you of everything I have said to you" (John 14:26).

Before reading the Bible, pray and invite God to speak to you. Don't go to Scripture looking for your idea, but go searching for his.

Not only should you read the Bible prayerfully, but you should also read it carefully. *"Seek and you will find"* is the pledge. The Bible is not a newspaper to be skimmed but rather a mine to be quarried. *"If you look for it as for silver and search for it as for hidden treasure, then you will understand the fear of the* LORD *and find the knowledge of God"* (Proverbs 2:4–5).

Any worthy find requires effort. The Bible is no exception. To understand the Bible, you don't have to be brilliant, but you must be willing to roll up your sleeves and search.

"Do your best to present yourself to God as one approved, a worker who does not need to be ashamed and who correctly handles the word of truth" (2 Timothy 2:15).

Here's a practical point. Study the Bible a bit at a time. Hunger is not satisfied by eating twenty-one meals in one sitting once a week. The body needs a steady diet to remain strong. So does the soul. When God sent food to his people in the wilderness, he didn't provide loaves already made. Instead, he sent them manna in the shape of *"thin flakes like frost on the ground"* (Exodus 16:14).

God gave manna in limited portions.

God sends spiritual food the same way. He opens the heavens with just enough nutrients for today's hunger. He provides *"a rule for this, a rule for that; a little here, a little there"* (Isaiah 28:10).

Don't be discouraged if your reading reaps a small harvest. Some days a lesser portion is all that is needed. What is important is to search every day for that day's message. A steady diet of God's Word over a lifetime builds a healthy soul and mind.

It's much like the little girl who returned from her first day at school feeling a bit dejected. Her mom asked, "Did you learn anything?"

"Apparently not enough," the girl responded. "I have to go back tomorrow, and the next day, and the next . . . "

Such is the case with learning. And such is the case with Bible study. Understanding comes little by little over a lifetime.

There is a third step in understanding the Bible. After the asking and seeking comes the knocking. After you ask and search, *"knock and the door will be opened to you"* (Matthew 7:7).

To knock is to stand at God's door. To make yourself available. To climb the steps, cross the porch, stand at the doorway, and volunteer. Knocking goes beyond the realm of thinking and into the realm of acting.

To knock is to ask, *What can I do? How can I obey? Where can I go?*

It's one thing to know what to do. It's another to do it. But for those who do it—those who choose to obey—a special reward awaits them.

"Whoever looks intently into the perfect law that gives freedom, and continues in it—not forgetting what they have heard, but doing it—they will be blessed in what they do" (James 1:25).

What a promise. Blessings come to those who do what they read in God's Word! It's the same with medicine. If you only read the label but ignore the pills, it won't help. It's the same with food. If you only read the recipe but never cook, you won't be fed. And it's the same with the Bible. If you only read the words but never obey, you'll never know the joy God has promised.

Ask. Search. Knock. Simple, isn't it? So why don't you give it a try? If you do, you'll see why the Bible is the most remarkable book in history.

INTRODUCTION TO
The Books of Ezra and Nehemiah

EZRA

Martin Luther you've heard of. Philipp Melanchthon, probably not. But Luther knew Melanchthon. And Luther was a better man as a result.

Melanchthon was the intellectual of the Reformation. He authored the Augsburg Confession. He was the first to put into writing an evangelical theology. He was only eleven when his father died, only twelve when his grandfather presented him with a Bible and a Greek grammar. The next fifty years the three were inseparable.

Melanchthon's one great love was to teach the Word of God. He didn't just read the Bible; he devoured it. By the age of seventeen he was a faculty member at the University of Wittenberg. Though he was small of frame and frail of health, he was keen of mind. And even more important, he was keen of purpose.

He lived to study and teach the Bible. He commanded the respect of Martin Luther. "I was born to fight," he said, "but Master Philipp, he comes along sowing with joy."

The prophet Ezra was the Philipp Melanchthon of his day. Ezra was the second of three key leaders to leave Babylon for the reconstruction of Jerusalem. Zerubbabel was first. Then Ezra and then Nehemiah. Zerubbabel reconstructed the temple, Nehemiah rebuilt the walls, and Ezra restored the worship.

Any person who has tackled the task of presenting the Bible to people will find a friend in Ezra. He was a student. He was an interpreter. In fact, the clearest Old Testament reference to exposition is attributed to Ezra. He was the head of the Levites who "read distinctly from the book, in the Law of God; and they gave the sense, and helped them to understand the reading" (Nehemiah 8:8 NKJV).

Don't you appreciate that last phrase, "gave the sense, and helped them to understand . . ."? Don't you appreciate the person who can take the Word and reveal it for your life?

Perhaps you can do that. If so, stay faithful. There is no higher task.

Perhaps you have a teacher like that. If so, be grateful. There is no greater friend.

AUTHOR AND DATE

Ezra was a priest and a scribe who lived during the time of the Babylonian captivity. He was the son of Seraiah (see Ezra 7:1), the last high priest to serve in the First Temple (see 2 Kings 25:18), and a descendant of Hilkah, the high priest who had found a copy of the Book of the Law during the reign of Josiah (see 2 Chronicles 34:14). Ezra would have been unable to perform his functions as a priest during the captivity, so instead he devoted his time to studying the Hebrew Scriptures and becoming "a teacher well versed in the Law of Moses" (Ezra 7:6). It is believed that Ezra also wrote the books of 1 and 2 Chronicles and either compiled or edited the book of Nehemiah. Each of these works were likely composed from c. 450–500 BC.

SITUATION

In c. 605 BC, the Babylonian king Nebuchadnezzar invaded the nation of Judah and began carrying the Jewish people into exile. God had told his people (through the prophets) this would occur as a result of their unfaithfulness, but he had also promised they would begin to return after seventy years of captivity. This began in 539 BC when the Persian king Cyrus the Great overthrew the Babylonians and allowed the Jewish people to begin returning home in waves. A man named Zerubbabel led the first group home c. 538 BC (see Ezra 1–6). Ezra led the second group c. 458 BC (see Ezra 7–10), and at that time he organized the synagogue, founded the order of scribes, and helped settle the canon of Scripture and arrange the Psalms. Nehemiah led the third group home c. 445 BC during the reign of King Artaxerxes I of Persia (see Nehemiah 1–12).

KEY THEMES

- When the Hebrews were allowed to return home their spiritual restoration was as important as their national restoration.
- Restoring the temple was a significant step in the spiritual restoration of the people.
- The idolatry of the Hebrews was rooted in foreign wives who continued to worship their false gods. This is why the men were asked to divorce their foreign wives.

KEY VERSES

For Ezra had devoted himself to the study and observance of the Law of the LORD, and to teaching its decrees and laws in Israel (Ezra 7:10).

CONTENTS

NEHEMIAH

You are about to meet the Abraham Lincoln of the Old Testament. A respected leader with a tender heart. You will see his tears in the oval office as he weeps for people oppressed and vulnerable.

You are about to meet the General George Patton of the Old Testament. A rugged leader. Intolerant of compromise. Relentless in demanding perfection. He punished those who were soft by pushing them down and cursing their names.

You are about to meet the Winston Churchill of the Old Testament. A statesman. Tested and tried. Resisting the enemies who seek to lure him away from the task. Rising above the squabbling factions who could distract him.

The tenderness of Lincoln. The fire of Patton. The savvy of Churchill. All found in the same man. Nehemiah.

When we meet him he is wearing the robe of royalty. He is the king's cupbearer. But though he was in a position of power, his heart beat for people in Israel. He was a Hebrew in Persia. When word reached him that the Temple was being reconstructed, he grew anxious. He knew there was no wall to protect it.

Nehemiah invited God to use him to save the city. God answered his prayer by softening the heart of the Persian king. Artaxerxes gave not only his blessing, but also supplies to be used in the project.

Nehemiah exchanged the royal robe for coveralls and got to work. The project took twelve years and was uphill all the way. He was accused of everything from allowing faulty construction to being power-hungry. In spite of grumpy workers and lurking enemies, he made it. With the wall built and the enemy silent, the people rejoiced and Nehemiah went back to Persia.

After twelve years he returned. The walls were strong, but the people had gone to pot. Faith was forgotten and discipline was a bad word. So Nehemiah got busy again.

He went to his closet, hung up his royal robe, bypassed his coveralls, and dusted off his frock and set about the task of teaching the people a few things about morality. He didn't mince words. "I contended with them and cursed them, struck some of them and pulled out their hair" (13:25 NKJV). Not what you'd call a typical Bible class.

But Nehemiah wasn't what you'd call a typical fellow.

AUTHOR AND DATE

Nehemiah was a "cupbearer" to the Persian king Artaxerxes I, who reigned c. 464–424 BC. In this role, Nehemiah was responsible for serving the drinks at the royal table and was trusted to guard the king against any plots to poison him. Nehemiah's position and close relationship with Artaxerxes thus enabled him to exert influence over the king and gain permission to lead a third wave of Jewish exiles home. Although the book is written from Nehemiah's perspective, it is believed the books of Ezra and Nehemiah were originally joined together as a single unit. Ezra likely thus compiled the book from Nehemiah's notes and memoirs, c. 450–500 BC.

SITUATION

As previously noted, Ezra led the second group of exiles back to Jerusalem c. 458 BC. Those who returned to Judah found their territory diminished and surrounded by antagonistic neighbors, and by 445 BC reports reached Nehemiah, who was living in the Persian city of Susa, that the walls of Jerusalem had not been rebuilt. Nehemiah appealed to Artaxerxes and was granted permission to lead a third wave of exiles back to their homeland. The events of Nehemiah chronicle the people's struggle to rebuild the wall in fifty-two days while under continual attack from outside enemies and internal squabbles—each of which threatened to derail the project. The final chapters of Nehemiah and the book of Malachi likely represent the last of the Old Testament writings, both in terms of the timing of events and date of composition.

KEY THEMES

- Nehemiah was grieved that his homeland wasn't being resettled quickly.
- Nehemiah faced opposition in building the wall, but he overcame it through organization and the loyalty of his countrymen.
- Nehemiah dedicated the wall to the Lord before he returned to Babylon.

KEY VERSES

They read from the Book of the Law of God, making it clear and giving the meaning so that the people understood what was being read (Nehemiah 8:8).

CONTENTS

FOLLOWING GOD'S GUIDANCE

Then the heads of the fathers' houses of Judah and Benjamin, and the priests and the Levites, with all whose spirits God had moved, arose to go up and build the house of the LORD.
EZRA 1:5 NKJV

REFLECTION

Think of a time when you felt God calling you to do something and you acted on that prompting. What blessings did you experience as a result of your obedience?

_____

_____

_____

SITUATION

Following the reign of King Solomon, the unified nation of Israel split into two parts—the larger kingdom of "Israel" in the north and the smaller kingdom of "Judah" in the south. While a few of the kings who would come to rule these nations were faithful to God, for the most part they led their people into idolatry and sin. As a result, God allowed the Assyrian Empire to conquer the nation of Israel in 722 BC and absorb its people into their culture. Judah lasted until c. 605 BC, when the Babylonians invaded, but this time God preserved the Jewish people in their exile. The events in Ezra take place approximately seventy years later, when the Persian king Cyrus the Great conquered the Babylonians and began to allow the people of Judah to return home.

OBSERVATION

Read Ezra 1:1–11 from the New International Version or the New King James Version.

NEW INTERNATIONAL VERSION
[1] In the first year of Cyrus king of Persia, in order to fulfill the word of the LORD spoken by Jeremiah, the LORD moved the heart of Cyrus king of Persia to make a proclamation throughout his realm and also to put it in writing:

[2] "This is what Cyrus king of Persia says:

"'The LORD, the God of heaven, has given me all the kingdoms of the earth and he has appointed me to build a temple for him at Jerusalem in Judah. [3] Any of his people among you may go up to Jerusalem in Judah and build the temple of the LORD, the God of Israel, the God who is in Jerusalem, and may their God be with them. [4] And in any locality where survivors may now be living, the people are to provide them with silver and gold, with goods and livestock, and with free-will offerings for the temple of God in Jerusalem.'"

[5] Then the family heads of Judah and Benjamin, and the priests and Levites—everyone whose heart God had moved—prepared to go up and build the house of the LORD in Jerusalem. [6] All their neighbors assisted them with articles of silver and gold, with goods and livestock, and with valuable gifts, in addition to all the freewill offerings.

[7] Moreover, King Cyrus brought out the articles belonging to the temple of the LORD, which Nebuchadnezzar had carried away from Jerusalem and had placed in the temple of his god. [8] Cyrus king of Persia had them brought by Mithredath the treasurer, who counted them out to Sheshbazzar the prince of Judah.

[9] This was the inventory:

gold dishes	300
silver dishes	1,000
silver pans	29
[10] gold bowls	30
matching silver bowls	410
other articles	1,000

[11] In all, there were 5,400 articles of gold and of silver. Sheshbazzar brought all these along with the exiles when they came up from Babylon to Jerusalem.

New King James Version

¹ Now in the first year of Cyrus king of Persia, that the word of the LORD by the mouth of Jeremiah might be fulfilled, the LORD stirred up the spirit of Cyrus king of Persia, so that he made a proclamation throughout all his kingdom, and also put it in writing, saying,

² Thus says Cyrus king of Persia:

All the kingdoms of the earth the LORD God of heaven has given me. And He has commanded me to build Him a house at Jerusalem which is in Judah. ³ Who is among you of all His people? May his God be with him, and let him go up to Jerusalem which is in Judah, and build the house of the LORD God of Israel (He is God), which is in Jerusalem. ⁴ And whoever is left in any place where he dwells, let the men of his place help him with silver and gold, with goods and livestock, besides the freewill offerings for the house of God which is in Jerusalem.

⁵ Then the heads of the fathers' houses of Judah and Benjamin, and the priests and the Levites, with all whose spirits God had moved, arose to go up and build the house of the LORD which is in Jerusalem. ⁶ And all those who were around them encouraged them with articles of silver and gold, with goods and livestock, and with precious things, besides all that was willingly offered.

⁷ King Cyrus also brought out the articles of the house of the LORD, which Nebuchadnezzar had taken from Jerusalem and put in the temple of his gods; ⁸ and Cyrus king of Persia brought them out by the hand of Mithredath the treasurer, and counted them out to Sheshbazzar the prince of Judah. ⁹ This is the number of them: thirty gold platters, one thousand silver platters, twenty-nine knives, ¹⁰ thirty gold basins, four hundred and ten silver basins of a similar kind, and one thousand other articles. ¹¹ All the articles of gold and silver were five thousand four hundred. All these Sheshbazzar took with the captives who were brought from Babylon to Jerusalem.

EXPLORATION

1. What do you think it means when Ezra writes that God "moved the heart of Cyrus" (verse 1) to issue the decree for the Jewish exiles to return home?

2. How did Cyrus, king of the greatest empire of the time, demonstrate humility before God?

3. Why are Cyrus's actions significant in light of the plight of the Jews?

4. What instructions did Cyrus give to the Jewish people?

5. Why was it important for the people who stayed behind to support those who were willing to go and work on the temple in Jerusalem?

_____

_____

_____

6. Why do you think Cyrus gave the articles from the temple that King Nebuchadnezzar had carried away back to the Jewish people?

_____

_____

_____

_____

INSPIRATION

You think it's hard to walk in the dark? Find it difficult to navigate a room with the lights off or your eyes closed? Try flying a small plane at 15,000 feet. Blind.

Jim O'Neill did. Not that he intended to do so. The sixty-five-year-old pilot was forty minutes into a four-hour solo flight from Glasgow, Scotland, to Colchester, England, when his vision failed. He initially thought he had been blinded by the sun but soon realized it was much worse. "Suddenly I couldn't see the dials in front of me. It was just a blur. I was helpless."

He gave new meaning to the phrase "flying blind."

Turns out, he'd suffered a stroke. O'Neill groped and found the radio of his Cessna and issued a Mayday alert. Paul Gerrard, a Royal Air Force Wing Commander who had just completed a training sortie nearby, was contacted by air traffic controllers and took off in O'Neill's direction. He found the plane and began talking to the stricken pilot.

The commander told O'Neill what to do. His instructions were reassuring and simple: "A gentle right turn, please. Left a bit. Right a bit."

He hovered within five hundred feet of O'Neill, shepherding him toward the nearest runway. Upon reaching it, the two began to descend. When asked if he could see the runway below, O'Neill apologized, "No sir, negative." O'Neill would have to land the plane by faith, not by sight. He hit the runway but bounced up again. The same thing happened on the second attempt. But on the eighth try, the blinded pilot managed to make a near-perfect landing.

Can you empathize with O'Neill? Most can. We've been struck, perhaps not with a stroke, but with a divorce, a sick child, or a cancer-ridden body. Not midair, but midcareer, mid-semester, midlife. We've lost sight of any safe landing strip and, in desperation, issued our share of Mayday prayers. We know the fear of flying blind.

Unlike O'Neill, however, we hear more than one voice. Many voices besiege our cockpit. The talk show host urges us to worry. The New Age guru says to relax. The financial page forecasts a downturn. The pastor says pray; the professor says phooey. So many opinions! Lose weight. Eat low fat. Join our church. Try our crystals. It's enough to make you cover your ears and run. . . .

Oh, the voices. How do we select the right one? . . .

We have what Jim O'Neill had: the commander's voice to guide us home. Let's heed it, shall we? Let's issue the necessary Mayday prayer and follow the guidance that God sends. If so, we will hear what O'Neill heard.

BBC News made the recording of the final four minutes of the flight available. Listen and you'll hear the patient voice of a confident commander. "You've missed the runway this time . . . Let's start another gentle righthand turn . . . Keep the right turn coming . . . Roll out left . . . No need to worry . . . Roll out left. Left again, left again . . . Keep coming down . . . Turn left, turn left . . . Hey, no problem . . . Can you see the runway now? . . . So you cannot see the runway? . . . Keep coming down . . ."

And then finally, "You are safe to land."

I'm looking forward to hearing that final sentence someday. Aren't you? (From *More to Your Story* by Max Lucado.)

REACTION

7. What are some times in your life when you had to "land the plane by faith, not by sight"?

_____

_____

_____

_____

8. Why is it often difficult to step out in faith when you feel that God is leading you?

_____

_____

_____

_____

9. How have you learned to distinguish between the different "voices" when it comes to discerning whether God is asking you to take a certain action?

_____

_____

_____

_____

10. What do you learn from the example of the Jewish exiles who obeyed God's call make the journey back to Judah and start work on rebuilding the temple?

_____

_____

_____

_____

11. What are some ways that God communicates his will to you today?

_____

_____

_____

12. In what ways has God helped you accomplish the things he has asked you to do?

_____

_____

_____

LIFE LESSONS

One of the most amazing titles given to Cyrus, the Persian king, was "Messiah." Who would dare call an unbeliever like Cyrus by that title? None other than God himself: "This is what the Lord says to his *anointed*, to Cyrus" (Isaiah 45:1, emphasis added). The word *anointed*, which can be translated *Messiah*, refers to someone whom God selects to accomplish his redemption. In this case, God used Cyrus to direct the exiled Jews back to Jerusalem. Later, he would send his own Son to bring all who believe in him back into fellowship with him. The book of Ezra reveals that God is sovereign over all human affairs and can use anyone, anything, or any situation for his divine purposes. He can use all aspects of life to lead us back to him.

DEVOTION

Father, we want to be people who are willing to give up everything to follow you. Help us to see the most valuable things this world has to offer are worthless compared to the blessings you give to those who obey you. Open our ears to hear your voice and help us to obey you.

JOURNALING

What step of obedience do you feel God is calling you to make this week?

_____

_____

_____

_____

_____

_____

_____

_____

_____

_____

_____

_____

_____

_____

_____

_____

_____

_____

_____

FOR FURTHER READING

To complete the books of Ezra and Nehemiah during this twelve-part study, read Ezra 1:1–2:70. For more Bible passages on obeying God, read Joshua 24:14–15; Micah 6:6–8; Matthew 7:21–27; John 14:15–21; Acts 5:27–32; Romans 6:11–18; 1 Peter 1:13–14; and 1 John 3:19–24.

WALKING
IN FAITH

Despite their fear of the peoples around them,
they built the altar on its foundation and
sacrificed burnt offerings on it to the LORD.

EZRA 3:3

REFLECTION

Think of a time you took a step of faith when you didn't know what the outcome would be. What helped you to make the decision? What happened as a result of your action?

_____

_____

_____

_____

_____

_____

SITUATION

Ezra continues his chronicle of the Jewish exiles' return by listing the different groups who return to their homeland under the leadership of Zerubbabel. When they arrive in Jerusalem, many of the heads of the families gave offerings to fund the rebuilding of the temple. When the time comes to start the project, the exiles take a step of faith by first building the *altar* and offering sacrifices to God. Only then do the people turn to the work of organizing the building effort and laying the foundation for the house of God that was to come.

OBSERVATION

Read Ezra 3:1–11 from the New International Version or the New King James Version.

NEW INTERNATIONAL VERSION

[1] When the seventh month came and the Israelites had settled in their towns, the people assembled together as one in Jerusalem. [2] Then Joshua son of Jozadak and his fellow priests and Zerubbabel son of Shealtiel and

his associates began to build the altar of the God of Israel to sacrifice burnt offerings on it, in accordance with what is written in the Law of Moses the man of God. ³ Despite their fear of the peoples around them, they built the altar on its foundation and sacrificed burnt offerings on it to the LORD, both the morning and evening sacrifices. ⁴ Then in accordance with what is written, they celebrated the Festival of Tabernacles with the required number of burnt offerings prescribed for each day. ⁵ After that, they presented the regular burnt offerings, the New Moon sacrifices and the sacrifices for all the appointed sacred festivals of the LORD, as well as those brought as freewill offerings to the LORD. ⁶ On the first day of the seventh month they began to offer burnt offerings to the LORD, though the foundation of the LORD's temple had not yet been laid.

⁷ Then they gave money to the masons and carpenters, and gave food and drink and olive oil to the people of Sidon and Tyre, so that they would bring cedar logs by sea from Lebanon to Joppa, as authorized by Cyrus king of Persia.

⁸ In the second month of the second year after their arrival at the house of God in Jerusalem, Zerubbabel son of Shealtiel, Joshua son of Jozadak and the rest of the people (the priests and the Levites and all who had returned from the captivity to Jerusalem) began the work. They appointed Levites twenty years old and older to supervise the building of the house of the LORD. ⁹ Joshua and his sons and brothers and Kadmiel and his sons (descendants of Hodaviah) and the sons of Henadad and their sons and brothers—all Levites—joined together in supervising those working on the house of God.

¹⁰ When the builders laid the foundation of the temple of the LORD, the priests in their vestments and with trumpets, and the Levites (the sons of Asaph) with cymbals, took their places to praise the LORD, as prescribed by David king of Israel. ¹¹ With praise and thanksgiving they sang to the LORD:

"He is good;
    his love toward Israel endures forever."

And all the people gave a great shout of praise to the LORD, because the foundation of the house of the LORD was laid.

NEW KING JAMES VERSION

[1] And when the seventh month had come, and the children of Israel were in the cities, the people gathered together as one man to Jerusalem. [2] Then Jeshua the son of Jozadak and his brethren the priests, and Zerubbabel the son of Shealtiel and his brethren, arose and built the altar of the God of Israel, to offer burnt offerings on it, as it is written in the Law of Moses the man of God. [3] Though fear had come upon them because of the people of those countries, they set the altar on its bases; and they offered burnt offerings on it to the LORD, both the morning and evening burnt offerings. [4] They also kept the Feast of Tabernacles, as it is written, and offered the daily burnt offerings in the number required by ordinance for each day. [5] Afterwards they offered the regular burnt offering, and those for New Moons and for all the appointed feasts of the LORD that were consecrated, and those of everyone who willingly offered a freewill offering to the LORD. [6] From the first day of the seventh month they began to offer burnt offerings to the LORD, although the foundation of the temple of the LORD had not been laid. [7] They also gave money to the masons and the carpenters, and food, drink, and oil to the people of Sidon and Tyre to bring cedar logs from Lebanon to the sea, to Joppa, according to the permission which they had from Cyrus king of Persia.

[8] Now in the second month of the second year of their coming to the house of God at Jerusalem, Zerubbabel the son of Shealtiel, Jeshua the son of Jozadak, and the rest of their brethren the priests and the Levites, and all those who had come out of the captivity to Jerusalem, began work and appointed the Levites from twenty years old and above to oversee the work of the house of the LORD. [9] Then Jeshua with his sons and brothers, Kadmiel with his sons, and the sons of Judah, arose as one to oversee those working on the house of God: the sons of Henadad with their sons and their brethren the Levites.

[10] When the builders laid the foundation of the temple of the LORD, the priests stood in their apparel with trumpets, and the Levites, the sons of Asaph, with cymbals, to praise the LORD, according to the ordinance of David king of Israel. [11] And they sang responsively, praising and giving thanks to the LORD:

"For He is good,
For His mercy endures forever toward Israel."

Then all the people shouted with a great shout, when they praised the LORD, because the foundation of the house of the LORD was laid.

EXPLORATION

1. The Jews started building an altar almost immediately after they returned to their homeland. What does that say about their priorities?

2. In light of their actions, what had the exiles learned during their years in captivity?

3. What risks did the Jews take in building an altar and offering sacrifices to God?

4. Why do you think it was important to the exiles to publicly demonstrate their faith in God?

5. Why was it important for the people to give to support the work on the temple?

6. Why did they celebrate completion of the temple's foundation?

_____

_____

_____

_____

_____

INSPIRATION

A few years ago, I took up road biking as a hobby and exercise. I bought the helmet, gloves, and thin-wheeled bike. I clipped my shoes in the pedals and almost died on the first ride. Hills are Everestish for the old and overweight. I literally had to walk my bike home.

Pat McGrath, a friend of mine, heard of my interest and offered to ride with me. Pat prefers biking to breathing. To him, biking _is_ breathing. If he didn't have a job and five kids, the Tour de France might have known one more American. He has pistons for legs and a locomotive engine for a heart. When I complained about the steep roads and stiff winds, he made this offer: "No problem. You can ride on my wheel."

To ride on a biker's wheel is to draft on him. When Pat and I pedal into a stiff wind, I pull in behind him as close as I dare. My front wheel is within a foot of his rear one. He vanguards into the breeze, leaving me a cone of calm in which to ride. And when we bike up stiff hills? I'm a bit embarrassed to admit this, but Pat has been known to place a hand on my back and push me up the incline.

Couldn't you use such a friend? You have one. When you place your faith in Christ, Christ places his Spirit before, behind, and within you. Not a strange spirit, but the same Spirit . . . . Everything Jesus did for his followers, his Spirit does for you. Jesus taught; the Spirit teaches. Jesus healed; the Spirit heals. Jesus comforted; his Spirit comforts. As Jesus sends you into new seasons, he sends his Counselor to go with you. . . .

God never sends you out alone. Are you on the eve of change? Do you find yourself looking into a new chapter? Is the foliage of your world showing signs of a new season? Heaven's message for you is clear: when everything else changes, God's presence never does. (From *Fearless* by Max Lucado.)

REACTION

7. What is a current situation in your life that is requiring you to place your faith in God?

_____

_____

_____

_____

8. How in that situation have you seen God "push you up the incline" as you trusted in him?

_____

_____

_____

_____

9. In what other ways have you seen God honor your faith when you trusted in him?

_____

_____

_____

_____

10. When are some times you have been tempted to not trust in him?

_____

_____

_____

11. What "new season" do you sense that God has for you in the near future? How are you seeking the leading of the Holy Spirit in that season?

_____

_____

_____

12. How can you help others in your life overcome their fear of a new season they are facing and put their trust completely in God?

_____

_____

_____

LIFE LESSONS

The returned Jewish exiles were ecstatic. They had taken a first step of faith, and now—after seventy years of captivity—they were again in their own land, in their own city, and were free to worship their Lord. The years of exile had taught them a lesson in faithfulness, and their first priority was now to build the altar and lay the foundation of the temple to demonstrate they would love the Lord with all their heart, soul, mind, and strength. God asks the same of us today—to "love the Lord your God will all your heart and with all your soul and with all your strength and with all your mind" (Luke 10:27). He has a great future in store for us. We just need to trust in his plans and take the first small step as he directs our path.

DEVOTION

Father, we cherish your presence with us. You are always near and always ready to take us back when we have turned away from you. Forgive us, Father, for thinking we don't need you. Help us to be faithful in good times and bad. Give us the courage to tell the world you are our God.

JOURNALING

What small step of faith are you willing to take today to demonstrate your trust in God?

_____

_____

_____

_____

_____

_____

_____

_____

_____

_____

_____

_____

_____

_____

_____

_____

FOR FURTHER READING

To complete the books of Ezra and Nehemiah during this twelve-part study, read Ezra 3:1–4:24. For more Bible passages on living by faith, read Genesis 15:1–6; 2 Chronicles 20:18–23; Proverbs 3:5–6; Matthew 9:27–31; Acts 15:6–11; 2 Corinthians 5:6–10; and Hebrews 11:1–2.

CELEBRATING GOD'S GOODNESS

*Then the children of Israel, the priests and the Levites
and the rest of the descendants of the captivity, celebrated
the dedication of this house of God with joy.*
EZRA 6:16 NKJV

REFLECTION

When was a time in your life that you celebrated something God had done for you?

_____

_____

_____

_____

_____

SITUATION

When the first wave of exiles return to Jerusalem, they discover that other people groups have settled into the region. These groups, concerned about losing their territory and influence, send a letter to the current Persian king to warn him about the "danger" the Jewish exiles pose. The king heeds their advice and issues an edict that stops work on the temple for many years. Later, when King Darius I comes to power, God sends the prophets Haggai and Zechariah to encourage the people the resume the work. The Jewish exiles appeal to Darius reminding him that King Cyrus had originally issued the decree to allow them to rebuild the house of God.

OBSERVATION

Read Ezra 6:13–22 from the New International Version or the New King James Version.

NEW INTERNATIONAL VERSION

[13] Then, because of the decree King Darius had sent, Tattenai, governor of Trans-Euphrates, and Shethar-Bozenai and their associates carried

it out with diligence. [14] So the elders of the Jews continued to build and prosper under the preaching of Haggai the prophet and Zechariah, a descendant of Iddo. They finished building the temple according to the command of the God of Israel and the decrees of Cyrus, Darius and Artaxerxes, kings of Persia. [15] The temple was completed on the third day of the month Adar, in the sixth year of the reign of King Darius.

[16] Then the people of Israel—the priests, the Levites and the rest of the exiles—celebrated the dedication of the house of God with joy. [17] For the dedication of this house of God they offered a hundred bulls, two hundred rams, four hundred male lambs and, as a sin offering for all Israel, twelve male goats, one for each of the tribes of Israel. [18] And they installed the priests in their divisions and the Levites in their groups for the service of God at Jerusalem, according to what is written in the Book of Moses.

[19] On the fourteenth day of the first month, the exiles celebrated the Passover. [20] The priests and Levites had purified themselves and were all ceremonially clean. The Levites slaughtered the Passover lamb for all the exiles, for their relatives the priests and for themselves. [21] So the Israelites who had returned from the exile ate it, together with all who had separated themselves from the unclean practices of their Gentile neighbors in order to seek the LORD, the God of Israel. [22] For seven days they celebrated with joy the Festival of Unleavened Bread, because the LORD had filled them with joy by changing the attitude of the king of Assyria so that he assisted them in the work on the house of God, the God of Israel.

NEW KING JAMES VERSION

[13] Then Tattenai, governor of the region beyond the River, Shethar-Boznai, and their companions diligently did according to what King Darius had sent. [14] So the elders of the Jews built, and they prospered through the prophesying of Haggai the prophet and Zechariah the son of Iddo. And they built and finished it, according to the commandment of the God of Israel, and according to the command of Cyrus, Darius, and

Artaxerxes king of Persia. ¹⁵ Now the temple was finished on the third day of the month of Adar, which was in the sixth year of the reign of King Darius. ¹⁶ Then the children of Israel, the priests and the Levites and the rest of the descendants of the captivity, celebrated the dedication of this house of God with joy. ¹⁷ And they offered sacrifices at the dedication of this house of God, one hundred bulls, two hundred rams, four hundred lambs, and as a sin offering for all Israel twelve male goats, according to the number of the tribes of Israel. ¹⁸ They assigned the priests to their divisions and the Levites to their divisions, over the service of God in Jerusalem, as it is written in the Book of Moses.

¹⁹ And the descendants of the captivity kept the Passover on the fourteenth day of the first month. ²⁰ For the priests and the Levites had purified themselves; all of them were ritually clean. And they slaughtered the Passover lambs for all the descendants of the captivity, for their brethren the priests, and for themselves. ²¹ Then the children of Israel who had returned from the captivity ate together with all who had separated themselves from the filth of the nations of the land in order to seek the Lord God of Israel. ²² And they kept the Feast of Unleavened Bread seven days with joy; for the Lord made them joyful, and turned the heart of the king of Assyria toward them, to strengthen their hands in the work of the house of God, the God of Israel.

EXPLORATION

1. What factors contributed to the success of the Jewish exiles' building efforts?

2. Read Haggai 2:2–5 and Zechariah 8:2–8. How would the words of these prophets served to encourage the people of Israel during this time?

3. Why did the people commemorate the completion of the temple?

4. What did some people give up in order to worship the God of Israel?

5. Why was it important for the people to install priests to serve in the temple?

6. Why was it important for the people to again celebrate the feasts of the Lord?

INSPIRATION

John Wesley wrote, "Sing lustily, and with a good courage. Beware of singing as if you were half dead, or half asleep; but lift up your voice with strength. Be no more afraid of your voice now, nor more ashamed of its being heard, than when you sung the songs of Satan."

Speaking of Satan, he cannot tolerate Christ-centered worship. Unlike God, he is not omniscient. Satan cannot read your mind. He is not moved by what you think, only by what you say. So say it! "Yell a loud no to the Devil and watch him scamper. Say a quiet yes to God and he'll be there in no time" (James 4:7–8 MSG).

Do you want your city to be free from Satan's grip? Worship! Do you want your home to be loosed from the devil? Worship! Do we want nations to be places of peace and prosperity? Then let the church assault Satan's strongholds with joy-filled praise.

Worship verbally . . . and worship in community. "There was . . . a *multitude* of the heavenly host praising God" (Luke 2:13 NKJV, emphasis added). The presence of Christ deserves an abundant chorus.

Every generation has its share of "Jesus, yes; church, no" Christians. For a variety of reasons, they turn away from church attendance. They do so at a great loss. Something happens in corporate worship that does not happen in private worship. When you see my face in the sanctuary and I hear your voice in the chorus, we are mutually edified.

Granted, congregational worship is imperfect. We often sing off-key. Our attention tends to wander. The preacher stumbles over his words, and the organist misses her cue. Even so, let us worship. The sincerity of our worship matters more than the quality. "Let's see how inventive we can be in encouraging love and helping out, not avoiding worshiping together as some do but spurring each other on, especially as we see the big Day approaching" (Hebrews 10:24–25 MSG). . . .

Let your body express what your heart is feeling. And let your heart be awakened by your body. "May the lifting up of my hands be like the evening sacrifice" (Psalm 141:2). "Because your love is better than life, my lips will glorify you. I will praise you as long as I live, and in your name I will lift up my hands" (Psalm 63:3–4). (From *Because of Bethlehem* by Max Lucado.)

REACTION

7. Why is it important to worship God if you want to see Satan's plans thwarted on earth?

_____

_____

_____

_____

8. Why is it critical to gather with others and worship God?

_____

_____

_____

9. What does the example of the Jewish exiles reveal about celebrating even the small things that God has done for you?

_____

_____

_____

10. What are some small victories in your life that you can thank God for today?

_____

_____

_____

_____

11. What are some things that tend to interfere with our worship to God?

_____

_____

_____

12. How can you encourage others to look for God's blessings in their lives and praise him for those victories?

_____

_____

LIFE LESSONS

All too often, those of us in the church tend to get caught up in "worship preferences." We don't like the way the person up front is leading the congregation in worship. We're tired of singing the same songs. We don't prefer hearing them played on guitar. The music is too upbeat . . . or not upbeat enough. The reality is that God calls us to worship at all times, in all places, and in a variety of ways: "with the sounding of the trumpet . . . the harp and lyre . . . timbrel and dancing . . . strings and pipe . . . resounding cymbals" (Psalm 150:3–5). God loves the joyful variety of worship expressions. And what he cares about most is not the _way_ that we worship but the fact that we are _actually worshiping_ him.

DEVOTION

Father, thank you for all of your many blessings—both great and small. We praise you today for all you have done and ask you to teach us each day what it means to truly worship you with our lives. Deepen our understanding and appreciation or what you have done so that we may continually give you the praise and adoration you deserve.

JOURNALING

What are some reasons you have today to celebrate and worship God?

FOR FURTHER READING

To complete the books of Ezra and Nehemiah during this twelve-part study, read Ezra 5:1–6:22. For more Bible passages on worshiping God, read Exodus 15:1–18; 2 Kings 17:36–39; 1 Chronicles 16:28–29; Psalm 95:1–7; John 4:21–24; Romans 12:1–2; Colossians 3:14–17; and Hebrews 13:15–16.

TRUSTING IN GOD'S PROTECTION

*The hand of our God was on us, and he protected
us from enemies and bandits along the way.*
EZRA 8:31

REFLECTION

What are some recent ways you have experienced God's protection or provision?

_____

_____

_____

_____

SITUATION

The years pass, and another Persian king comes to power. It is this monarch, Artaxerxes I, who grants Ezra permission to lead a second wave of exiles home in c. 458 BC, and he even graciously provides resources to restart the building of the temple. Ezra lists the family groups who will be a part of this migration, but he encounters a problem—there are no Levites (priestly class) to lead the people in worship. Ezra appeals to the local leaders, and soon twenty Levites agree to join the group. Following this, Ezra gathers the exiles near the banks of the Euphrates River in Babylon and proclaims a time of prayer and fasting for the upcoming journey.

OBSERVATION

Read Ezra 8:21–32 from the New International Version or the New King James Version.

New International Version

21 There, by the Ahava Canal, I proclaimed a fast, so that we might humble ourselves before our God and ask him for a safe journey for us and our children, with all our possessions. 22 I was ashamed to ask

the king for soldiers and horsemen to protect us from enemies on the road, because we had told the king, "The gracious hand of our God is on everyone who looks to him, but his great anger is against all who forsake him." [23] So we fasted and petitioned our God about this, and he answered our prayer.

[24] Then I set apart twelve of the leading priests, namely, Sherebiah, Hashabiah and ten of their brothers, [25] and I weighed out to them the offering of silver and gold and the articles that the king, his advisers, his officials and all Israel present there had donated for the house of our God. [26] I weighed out to them 650 talents of silver, silver articles weighing 100 talents, 100 talents of gold, [27] 20 bowls of gold valued at 1,000 darics, and two fine articles of polished bronze, as precious as gold.

[28] I said to them, "You as well as these articles are consecrated to the LORD. The silver and gold are a freewill offering to the LORD, the God of your ancestors. [29] Guard them carefully until you weigh them out in the chambers of the house of the LORD in Jerusalem before the leading priests and the Levites and the family heads of Israel." [30] Then the priests and Levites received the silver and gold and sacred articles that had been weighed out to be taken to the house of our God in Jerusalem.

[31] On the twelfth day of the first month we set out from the Ahava Canal to go to Jerusalem. The hand of our God was on us, and he protected us from enemies and bandits along the way. [32] So we arrived in Jerusalem, where we rested three days.

NEW KING JAMES VERSION

[21] Then I proclaimed a fast there at the river of Ahava, that we might humble ourselves before our God, to seek from Him the right way for us and our little ones and all our possessions. [22] For I was ashamed to request of the king an escort of soldiers and horsemen to help us against the enemy on the road, because we had spoken to the king, saying, "The hand of our God is upon all those for good who seek Him, but His power and His wrath are against all those who forsake Him." [23] So we fasted and entreated our God for this, and He answered our prayer.

²⁴ And I separated twelve of the leaders of the priests—Sherebiah, Hashabiah, and ten of their brethren with them— ²⁵ and weighed out to them the silver, the gold, and the articles, the offering for the house of our God which the king and his counselors and his princes, and all Israel who were present, had offered. ²⁶ I weighed into their hand six hundred and fifty talents of silver, silver articles weighing one hundred talents, one hundred talents of gold, ²⁷ twenty gold basins worth a thousand drachmas, and two vessels of fine polished bronze, precious as gold. ²⁸ And I said to them, "You are holy to the LORD; the articles are holy also; and the silver and the gold are a freewill offering to the LORD God of your fathers. ²⁹ Watch and keep them until you weigh them before the leaders of the priests and the Levites and heads of the fathers' houses of Israel in Jerusalem, in the chambers of the house of the LORD." ³⁰ So the priests and the Levites received the silver and the gold and the articles by weight, to bring them to Jerusalem to the house of our God.

³¹ Then we departed from the river of Ahava on the twelfth day of the first month, to go to Jerusalem. And the hand of our God was upon us, and He delivered us from the hand of the enemy and from ambush along the road. ³² So we came to Jerusalem, and stayed there three days.

EXPLORATION

1. Why do you think Ezra began the journey by asking the people to fast and humble themselves before God?

_____

_____

2. Why was Ezra "afraid" to ask the king for soldiers and horsemen to protect them?

_____

_____

3. How did Ezra demonstrate that he had complete confidence in God's protection?

4. Why was it critical that the silver, gold, and other articles reached Jerusalem?

5. In what ways did God answer the prayers of the Israelites?

6. What does this passage reveal to you about trusting in God and taking steps of faith?

INSPIRATION

God is unchanging. The weather changes. Fashion changes. Even change changes. God has not changed and cannot and will not ever change. He is always the same—yesterday, today, and tomorrow (see Hebrews 6:17–18).

God is unparalleled. Nobody comes close to his power, creativity, wisdom, or love. Many arrogantly believe they are close, but all fall short. There is no one like him (see Isaiah 40:13–14).

God is ungoverned. You and I have policemen, security guards, politicians, and homeowners' association board members telling us what to do. Not God. He holds the position of King of all kings (see 1 Timothy 6:15–16).

God is unbelievable. Writers (like myself) try to encapsulate God with a thesaurus of adjectives, but still our fingers freeze up on the keyboard (as mine are now). He's just so . . . well . . . (see Job 11:7–8).

God is untouched. One wayward sneeze in my direction, and I am contaminated, sick with a cold and out for a week. No one can soil or stain God. No outbreak of sin can contaminate him. God is holy and righteous, no matter how sick the world gets (see 1 Samuel 2:2).

God is uncaused. God has no "Made in . . ." stickers on his side. No birthday. No childhood. No influences listed on his résumé. Since no one put God in power, no one can take him out (see Psalm 90:1–2).

God is unlimited. We are limited by brain capacity, time, relationship overload, responsibilities (one can be at only one baseball practice at a time), and patience. God has no limit to his time, power, knowledge, and love (see Psalm 147:4–5).

So, can you rely on God to take care of you?

I'll let you answer that. (From *Max on Life* by Max Lucado.)

REACTION

7. When you look at everything the Bible says about God, how can you be assured that you can rely on the Lord completely to take care of you?

_____

_____

_____

8. What are some things that tend to inhibit your ability to trust God with your needs?

_____

_____

_____

9. How has God helped you to overcome these hindrances and trust more fully in him?

10. What message do you send to others when you trust God to help you?

11. How have you seen God prove to be faithful to you in the past?

12. How does remembering what God has done for you in the past influence your attitude toward your present needs?

LIFE LESSONS

There are so many things in life over which we have no control—especially when we set out on a trip. Accidents, bad weather, construction work, rush hours, delays, sickness, mechanical failures, missed connections . . . almost anything can happen. Ezra understood the dangers of travel in his day as well, which is why he instructed the people to first *fast and pray* for God's protection before they took their first step. Planning for trips serves a great reminder that while *we* can't control everything in our world, we serve a God who *is* in control of everything that happens and is ready to help us. As we seek his protection, we can confidently assert—as did the Jewish pilgrims on their way to Jerusalem—"My help comes from the LORD, the Maker of heaven and earth" (Psalm 121:2).

DEVOTION

Father, thank you for your constant care for us. You have proven time and time again that you are a loving father who always protects and provides for his children. Help us to put our full confidence in you and trust you with our daily needs. May we rest secure in your loving arms.

JOURNALING

In what area of your life do you need to trust God more for his protection?

FOR FURTHER READING

To complete the books of Ezra and Nehemiah during this twelve-part study, read Ezra 7:1–8:36. For more Bible passages on trusting God, read Joshua 1:7–9; Psalm 62:5–8; 143:7–10; Proverbs 29:25; Isaiah 25:6–9; Matthew 6:25–27; Luke 10:25–28; and Philippians 4:6–7.

DEALING WITH GUILT

*"O my God, I am too ashamed and humiliated
to lift up my face to You, my God; for our
iniquities have risen higher than our heads,
and our guilt has grown up to the heavens."*

Ezra 9:6 NKJV

REFLECTION

Think of a time when you experienced relief from a burden of guilt. What was the situation? What changed in your life as a result of the experience?

_____

_____

_____

_____

SITUATION

As Ezra prepares to lead the Jewish exiles back to Judah, he soon is made aware of another problem. "The people of Israel . . . have not kept themselves separate from the neighboring peoples with their detestable practices" (Ezra 9:1). Many of the Jewish people had also taken foreign spouses—sinful practices that had led the nation into captivity in the first place. Ezra is stunned by the news, and in response he gathers the people together to address the situation.

OBSERVATION

Read Ezra 9:1–15 from the New International
Version or the New King James Version.

NEW INTERNATIONAL VERSION
¹ After these things had been done, the leaders came to me and said, "The people of Israel, including the priests and the Levites, have not kept themselves separate from the neighboring peoples with their detestable practices, like those of the Canaanites, Hittites, Perizzites, Jebusites, Ammonites, Moabites, Egyptians and Amorites. ² They have taken

some of their daughters as wives for themselves and their sons, and have mingled the holy race with the peoples around them. And the leaders and officials have led the way in this unfaithfulness."

[3] When I heard this, I tore my tunic and cloak, pulled hair from my head and beard and sat down appalled. [4] Then everyone who trembled at the words of the God of Israel gathered around me because of this unfaithfulness of the exiles. And I sat there appalled until the evening sacrifice.

[5] Then, at the evening sacrifice, I rose from my self-abasement, with my tunic and cloak torn, and fell on my knees with my hands spread out to the LORD my God [6] and prayed:

"I am too ashamed and disgraced, my God, to lift up my face to you, because our sins are higher than our heads and our guilt has reached to the heavens. [7] From the days of our ancestors until now, our guilt has been great. Because of our sins, we and our kings and our priests have been subjected to the sword and captivity, to pillage and humiliation at the hand of foreign kings, as it is today.

[8] "But now, for a brief moment, the LORD our God has been gracious in leaving us a remnant and giving us a firm place in his sanctuary, and so our God gives light to our eyes and a little relief in our bondage. [9] Though we are slaves, our God has not forsaken us in our bondage. He has shown us kindness in the sight of the kings of Persia: He has granted us new life to rebuild the house of our God and repair its ruins, and he has given us a wall of protection in Judah and Jerusalem.

[10] "But now, our God, what can we say after this? For we have forsaken the commands [11] you gave through your servants the prophets when you said: 'The land you are entering to possess is a land polluted by the corruption of its peoples. By their detestable practices they have filled it with their impurity from one end to the other. [12] Therefore, do not give your daughters in marriage to their sons or take their daughters for your sons. Do not seek a treaty of friendship with them at any time, that you may be strong and eat the good

things of the land and leave it to your children as an everlasting inheritance.'

¹³ "What has happened to us is a result of our evil deeds and our great guilt, and yet, our God, you have punished us less than our sins deserved and have given us a remnant like this. ¹⁴ Shall we then break your commands again and intermarry with the peoples who commit such detestable practices? Would you not be angry enough with us to destroy us, leaving us no remnant or survivor? ¹⁵ LORD, the God of Israel, you are righteous! We are left this day as a remnant. Here we are before you in our guilt, though because of it not one of us can stand in your presence."

NEW KING JAMES VERSION

¹ When these things were done, the leaders came to me, saying, "The people of Israel and the priests and the Levites have not separated themselves from the peoples of the lands, with respect to the abominations of the Canaanites, the Hittites, the Perizzites, the Jebusites, the Ammonites, the Moabites, the Egyptians, and the Amorites. ² For they have taken some of their daughters as wives for themselves and their sons, so that the holy seed is mixed with the peoples of those lands. Indeed, the hand of the leaders and rulers has been foremost in this trespass." ³ So when I heard this thing, I tore my garment and my robe, and plucked out some of the hair of my head and beard, and sat down astonished. ⁴ Then everyone who trembled at the words of the God of Israel assembled to me, because of the transgression of those who had been carried away captive, and I sat astonished until the evening sacrifice.

⁵ At the evening sacrifice I arose from my fasting; and having torn my garment and my robe, I fell on my knees and spread out my hands to the LORD my God. ⁶ And I said: "O my God, I am too ashamed and humiliated to lift up my face to You, my God; for our iniquities have risen higher than our heads, and our guilt has grown up to the heavens. ⁷ Since the days of our fathers to this day we have been very guilty, and for our iniquities we, our kings, and our priests have been delivered into

the hand of the kings of the lands, to the sword, to captivity, to plunder, and to humiliation, as it is this day. [8] And now for a little while grace has been shown from the LORD our God, to leave us a remnant to escape, and to give us a peg in His holy place, that our God may enlighten our eyes and give us a measure of revival in our bondage. [9] For we were slaves. Yet our God did not forsake us in our bondage; but He extended mercy to us in the sight of the kings of Persia, to revive us, to repair the house of our God, to rebuild its ruins, and to give us a wall in Judah and Jerusalem. [10] And now, O our God, what shall we say after this? For we have forsaken Your commandments, [11] which You commanded by Your servants the prophets, saying, 'The land which you are entering to possess is an unclean land, with the uncleanness of the peoples of the lands, with their abominations which have filled it from one end to another with their impurity. [12] Now therefore, do not give your daughters as wives for their sons, nor take their daughters to your sons; and never seek their peace or prosperity, that you may be strong and eat the good of the land, and leave it as an inheritance to your children forever.' [13] And after all that has come upon us for our evil deeds and for our great guilt, since You our God have punished us less than our iniquities deserve, and have given us such deliverance as this, [14] should we again break Your commandments, and join in marriage with the people committing these abominations? Would You not be angry with us until You had consumed us, so that there would be no remnant or survivor? [15] O LORD God of Israel, You are righteous, for we are left as a remnant, as it is this day. Here we are before You, in our guilt, though no one can stand before You because of this!"

EXPLORATION

1. Why did the Jewish leaders feel compelled to bring their problem to Ezra's attention?

2. Why do you think Ezra reacted so strongly to the news?

_____

_____

_____

_____

3. Who shared in Ezra's remorse for the people's unfaithfulness to God?

_____

_____

_____

4. What was Ezra's initial response to the people's sin?

_____

_____

_____

5. Why did Ezra include himself in his prayer of repentance—even though he (and many others) had remained faithful to God?

_____

_____

_____

6. Why was it difficult for the Israelites to remember God's mercy and justice?

_____

_____

_____

INSPIRATION

Satan numbs our awareness and short-circuits our self-control. We know what we are doing, and yet can't believe that we are doing it. In the fog of weakness we want to stop but haven't the will to do so. We want to turn around, but our feet won't move. We want to run and, pitifully, we want to stay. . . .

Confusion. Guilt. Rationalization. Despair. It all hits. It hits hard. We numbly pick ourselves up and stagger back into our world. "Oh, God, what have I done?" "Should I tell someone?" "I'll never do it again." "My God, can you forgive me?"

No one who is reading these words is free from the treachery of sudden sin. No one is immune to this trick of perdition. This demon of hell can scale the highest monastery wall, penetrate the deepest faith, and desecrate the purest home.

Some of you know exactly what I mean. You could write these words better than I, couldn't you? Some of you, like me, have tumbled so often that the stench of Satan's breath is far from a novelty. You've asked for God's forgiveness so often that you worry that the well of mercy might run dry. . . .

Romans chapter 7 is the Emancipation Proclamation for those of us who have a tendency to tumble. Look at verse 15: "I do not understand what I do. For what I want to do I do not do, but what I hate I do."

Sound familiar? Read on. Verses 18–19: "For I have the desire to do what is good, but I cannot carry it out. For I do not do the good I want to do, but the evil I do not want to do—this I keep on doing."

Man, that fellow has been reading my diary! "What a wretched man I am! Who will rescue me from this body that is subject to death?"(verse 24).

Please, Paul, don't stop there! Is there no oasis in this barrenness of guilt? There is. Thank God and drink deeply as you read verse 25 and verse 1 of chapter 8: "Thanks be to God, who delivers me through Jesus Christ our Lord! . . . Therefore, there is now no condemnation for those who are in Christ Jesus."

Amen. There it is. You read it right. Underline it if you wish. For those *in* Christ there is *no* condemnation. Absolutely none. Claim the promise. Memorize the words. Accept the cleansing. Throw out the guilt. Praise the Lord. (From *Shaped by God* by Max Lucado.)

REACTION

7. What do you think causes some people to believe God's "well of mercy" will run dry?

_____

_____

_____

_____

8. How do Paul's words in Romans 7:25 and 8:1 assure you that God does not condemn those who seek his forgiveness and turn from their sins?

_____

_____

_____

_____

9. What are some ways that you tend to handle guilt and shame?

_____

_____

_____

_____

10. What does the example of Ezra and Paul's words in Romans reveal about the correct way to handle your guilt?

_____

_____

_____

_____

11. Why is it often tempting to ignore a guilty conscience?

_____

_____

_____

_____

12. In what area do you still need to accept God's forgiveness?

_____

_____

_____

_____

LIFE LESSONS

Sin leads to only one result: death. Paul wrote, "The wages of sin is death" (Romans 6:23). James added, "After desire is conceived, it gives birth to sin; and sin, when it is full-grown, gives birth to death" (James 1:15). Sin is not to be taken lightly. Time and again, Jesus called out the Pharisees—a group who *claimed* they were following God's law—for their sinful ways. But time and again, he offered mercy to those who acknowledged their sins and were honest about their mistakes. The Bible is clear that Jesus frees us from the penalty of sin and liberates us from its power. We just need to be honest as well about our failings and repent to God—and then believe he has blotted out the record (see Isaiah 43:35).

DEVOTION

Father, we pray that you would help us to be sensitive to the conviction of the Holy Spirit. Help us to repent of sin quickly and never let it take root in our lives. Teach us to release our guilt to you and to forgive ourselves so we may not live in bondage to our failures. May we always be thankful for your mercy and grace.

JOURNALING

What are some ways that you need to change the way you respond to guilt?

_____

_____

_____

_____

_____

_____

_____

_____

_____

_____

_____

_____

_____

_____

_____

_____

_____

_____

_____

FOR FURTHER READING

To complete the books of Ezra and Nehemiah during this twelve-part study, read Ezra 9:1–15. For more Bible passages on dealing with guilt, read 2 Samuel 12:11–14; Psalm 32:1–5; 38:1–4; Isaiah 6:1–7; Jeremiah 2:22–35; Acts 3:17–26; Romans 8:1–4; Philippians 3:12–14; and 1 John 1:8–10.

TRUE REPENTANCE

While Ezra was praying and confessing . . . a large crowd of Israelites—men, women and children— gathered around him. They too wept bitterly.

EZRA 10:1

REFLECTION

Think of a time when you asked a friend to forgive you. How did it feel to receive forgiveness?

_____

_____

_____

_____

SITUATION

The sin the people of God had committed was great. However, as Ezra corporately confessed their sins, "weeping and throwing himself down" (Ezra 10:1) in their midst, the people all gathered around him an also began to weep. What follows is admission of the people's guilt . . . and a promise they will made amends to put themselves back into line with what God had instructed. When Ezra hears this response, he leads the people in making the reforms.

OBSERVATION

Read Ezra 10:1–17 from the New International Version or the New King James Version.

New International Version

¹ While Ezra was praying and confessing, weeping and throwing himself down before the house of God, a large crowd of Israelites—men, women and children—gathered around him. They too wept bitterly. ² Then Shekaniah son of Jehiel, one of the descendants of Elam, said to Ezra, "We have been unfaithful to our God by marrying foreign women from the peoples around us. But in spite of this, there is still hope for

Israel. ³ Now let us make a covenant before our God to send away all these women and their children, in accordance with the counsel of my lord and of those who fear the commands of our God. Let it be done according to the Law.⁴ Rise up; this matter is in your hands. We will support you, so take courage and do it."

⁵ So Ezra rose up and put the leading priests and Levites and all Israel under oath to do what had been suggested. And they took the oath. ⁶ Then Ezra withdrew from before the house of God and went to the room of Jehohanan son of Eliashib. While he was there, he ate no food and drank no water, because he continued to mourn over the unfaithfulness of the exiles.

⁷ A proclamation was then issued throughout Judah and Jerusalem for all the exiles to assemble in Jerusalem. ⁸ Anyone who failed to appear within three days would forfeit all his property, in accordance with the decision of the officials and elders, and would himself be expelled from the assembly of the exiles.

⁹ Within the three days, all the men of Judah and Benjamin had gathered in Jerusalem. And on the twentieth day of the ninth month, all the people were sitting in the square before the house of God, greatly distressed by the occasion and because of the rain. ¹⁰ Then Ezra the priest stood up and said to them, "You have been unfaithful; you have married foreign women, adding to Israel's guilt. ¹¹ Now honor the LORD, the God of your ancestors, and do his will. Separate yourselves from the peoples around you and from your foreign wives."

¹² The whole assembly responded with a loud voice: "You are right! We must do as you say. ¹³ But there are many people here and it is the rainy season; so we cannot stand outside. Besides, this matter cannot be taken care of in a day or two, because we have sinned greatly in this thing. ¹⁴ Let our officials act for the whole assembly. Then let everyone in our towns who has married a foreign woman come at a set time, along with the elders and judges of each town, until the fierce anger of our God in this matter is turned away from us." ¹⁵ Only Jonathan son of Asahel and Jahzeiah son of Tikvah, supported by Meshullam and Shabbethai the Levite, opposed this.

[16] So the exiles did as was proposed. Ezra the priest selected men who were family heads, one from each family division, and all of them designated by name. On the first day of the tenth month they sat down to investigate the cases, [17] and by the first day of the first month they finished dealing with all the men who had married foreign women.

NEW KING JAMES VERSION

[1] Now while Ezra was praying, and while he was confessing, weeping, and bowing down before the house of God, a very large assembly of men, women, and children gathered to him from Israel; for the people wept very bitterly. [2] And Shechaniah the son of Jehiel, one of the sons of Elam, spoke up and said to Ezra, "We have trespassed against our God, and have taken pagan wives from the peoples of the land; yet now there is hope in Israel in spite of this. [3] Now therefore, let us make a covenant with our God to put away all these wives and those who have been born to them, according to the advice of my master and of those who tremble at the commandment of our God; and let it be done according to the law. [4] Arise, for this matter is your responsibility. We also are with you. Be of good courage, and do it."

[5] Then Ezra arose, and made the leaders of the priests, the Levites, and all Israel swear an oath that they would do according to this word. So they swore an oath. [6] Then Ezra rose up from before the house of God, and went into the chamber of Jehohanan the son of Eliashib; and when he came there, he ate no bread and drank no water, for he mourned because of the guilt of those from the captivity.

[7] And they issued a proclamation throughout Judah and Jerusalem to all the descendants of the captivity, that they must gather at Jerusalem, [8] and that whoever would not come within three days, according to the instructions of the leaders and elders, all his property would be confiscated, and he himself would be separated from the assembly of those from the captivity.

[9] So all the men of Judah and Benjamin gathered at Jerusalem within three days. It was the ninth month, on the twentieth of the month; and

all the people sat in the open square of the house of God, trembling because of this matter and because of heavy rain. [10] Then Ezra the priest stood up and said to them, "You have transgressed and have taken pagan wives, adding to the guilt of Israel. [11] Now therefore, make confession to the LORD God of your fathers, and do His will; separate yourselves from the peoples of the land, and from the pagan wives."

[12] Then all the assembly answered and said with a loud voice, "Yes! As you have said, so we must do. [13] But there are many people; it is the season for heavy rain, and we are not able to stand outside. Nor is this the work of one or two days, for there are many of us who have transgressed in this matter. [14] Please, let the leaders of our entire assembly stand; and let all those in our cities who have taken pagan wives come at appointed times, together with the elders and judges of their cities, until the fierce wrath of our God is turned away from us in this matter." [15] Only Jonathan the son of Asahel and Jahaziah the son of Tikvah opposed this, and Meshullam and Shabbethai the Levite gave them support.

[16] Then the descendants of the captivity did so. And Ezra the priest, with certain heads of the fathers' households, were set apart by the fathers' households, each of them by name; and they sat down on the first day of the tenth month to examine the matter. [17] By the first day of the first month they finished questioning all the men who had taken pagan wives.

EXPLORATION

1. How did Ezra serve as a good example in helping the people realize the gravity of their sin?

_____

_____

_____

_____

_____

_____

2. How did the Jewish leaders respond when they heard Ezra's prayer?

3. What did the Jewish leaders immediately commit to do to resolve the situation?

4. In what ways did the people demonstrate they were truly sorry for their sins?

5. What steps did the Israelites take to restore their relationship with God?

6. Why was it important for the exiles to separate themselves from their non-Jewish spouses?

INSPIRATION

"*If* we confess our sins, he is faithful and just . . ." (1 John 1:19, emphasis added). The biggest word in Scripture just might be that two-letter one, *if.* For confessing sins—admitting failure—is exactly what prisoners of pride refuse to do.

You know the lingo: "Well, I may not be perfect, but I'm better than Hitler and certainly kinder than Idi Amin!"

"Me a sinner? Oh, sure, I get rowdy every so often, but I'm a pretty good ol' boy."

"Listen, I'm just as good as the next guy. I pay my taxes. I coach the Little League team. I even make donations to Red Cross. Why, God's probably proud to have somebody like me on his team."

Justification. Rationalization. Comparison. These are the tools of the jailbird. They sound good. They sound familiar. They even sound American. But in the kingdom, they sound hollow.

"Blessed are those who mourn . . ." (Matthew 5:4). To *mourn* for your sins is a natural outflow of poverty of spirit. The second beatitude should follow the first. But that's not always the case. Many deny their weakness. Many know they are wrong, yet pretend they are right. As a result, they never taste the exquisite sorrow of repentance. . . .

When you mourn, when you get to the point of sorrow for your sins, when you admit that you have no other option but to cast all your cares on him, and when there is truly no other name that you can call, then cast all your cares on him, for he is waiting in the midst of the storm. (From *The Applause of Heaven* by Max Lucado.)

REACTION

7. What is the problem with thinking you are "just as good as the next guy"?

8. What are some of the things that tend to get in the way of believers confessing their sins?

_____

_____

_____

_____

_____

9. How would you define true repentance for your sins?

_____

_____

_____

_____

_____

10. In what ways can unconfessed sin affect a person's relationship with God and others?

_____

_____

_____

_____

_____

11. Why do you think Jesus says "blessed are those who mourn" (Matthew 5:4) for their sins?

_____

_____

_____

_____

12. How will you express your thanks to God today for his gift of forgiveness?

_____

_____

_____

_____

_____

_____

_____

LIFE LESSONS

The consequences of sin can be hard to bear. We may feel sorrow, shame, guilt, and loss as a result of what we have done. But it's important for us to remember that those feelings alone do not constitute repentance. Expressing our sorrow finds its meaning as an act of repentance when we go on to take steps to turn from our sin and live in obedience to God. As Paul expressed it, "Godly sorrow brings repentance that leads to salvation and leaves no regret, but worldly sorrow brings death" (2 Corinthians 7:10). Repentance is confession of sin in working clothes. It must be intentional, honest, and open to facing the consequences of our actions—knowing all the while that God is readily forgiving us and lovingly restoring us.

DEVOTION

Father, we are unworthy to stand in your presence, yet through the blood of your Son we come to you for mercy. Remind us of the importance of repentance. Give us strength through your Holy Spirit to turn away from our sin. And show us how to deepen our relationship with you.

JOURNALING

Is there any area of your life in which you still need to repent?

_____

_____

_____

_____

_____

_____

_____

_____

_____

_____

_____

_____

_____

_____

_____

_____

_____

_____

_____

FOR FURTHER READING

To complete the books of Ezra and Nehemiah during this twelve-part study, read Ezra 10:1–44. For more Bible passages on repentance, read 2 Chronicles 7:11–14; Jeremiah 15:19–21; Ezekiel 18:30–32; Matthew 3:1–3; Acts 17:24–31; Romans 2:1–4; 2 Peter 3:8–9; and Revelation 2:4–6.

PRAYER AND ACTION

So it was, when I heard these words, that I sat down and wept, and mourned for many days; I was fasting and praying before the God of heaven.

NEHEMIAH 1:4 NKJV

REFLECTION

Think of a recent situation in your life that caused you to go to God immediately in prayer. What happened as a result of your prayer and action?

_____

_____

_____

_____

SITUATION

When the story of the Jewish exiles picks up in the book of Nehemiah (c. 446 BC), approximately twelve years have passed since Ezra led the second wave of people back to Judah. At the time, a man named Nehemiah—a cupbearer to the Persian king Artaxerxes I—is living in the citadel of Susa when he receives word that the second wave of exiles are not faring well. After all these years, the walls of Jerusalem still lie in ruin, and the people are being continually harassed by the enemies in the region. Nehemiah responds with grief... but also with prayer and action.

OBSERVATION

Read Nehemiah 1:1–11 from the New International Version or the New King James Version.

NEW INTERNATIONAL VERSION

¹ The words of Nehemiah son of Hakaliah:

In the month of Kislev in the twentieth year, while I was in the citadel of Susa, ² Hanani, one of my brothers, came from Judah with some other men, and I questioned them about the Jewish remnant that had survived the exile, and also about Jerusalem.

³ They said to me, "Those who survived the exile and are back in the province are in great trouble and disgrace. The wall of Jerusalem is broken down, and its gates have been burned with fire."

⁴ When I heard these things, I sat down and wept. For some days I mourned and fasted and prayed before the God of heaven. ⁵ Then I said:

"LORD, the God of heaven, the great and awesome God, who keeps his covenant of love with those who love him and keep his commandments, ⁶ let your ear be attentive and your eyes open to hear the prayer your servant is praying before you day and night for your servants, the people of Israel. I confess the sins we Israelites, including myself and my father's family, have committed against you. ⁷ We have acted very wickedly toward you. We have not obeyed the commands, decrees and laws you gave your servant Moses.

⁸ "Remember the instruction you gave your servant Moses, saying, 'If you are unfaithful, I will scatter you among the nations, ⁹ but if you return to me and obey my commands, then even if your exiled people are at the farthest horizon, I will gather them from there and bring them to the place I have chosen as a dwelling for my Name.'

¹⁰ "They are your servants and your people, whom you redeemed by your great strength and your mighty hand. ¹¹ Lord, let your ear be attentive to the prayer of this your servant and to the prayer of your servants who delight in revering your name. Give your servant success today by granting him favor in the presence of this man."

I was cupbearer to the king.

NEW KING JAMES VERSION

¹ The words of Nehemiah the son of Hachaliah.

It came to pass in the month of Chislev, in the twentieth year, as I was in Shushan the citadel, ² that Hanani one of my brethren came with men from Judah; and I asked them concerning the Jews who had escaped, who had survived the captivity, and concerning Jerusalem. ³ And they said to me, "The survivors who are left from the captivity in the province are there in great distress and reproach. The wall of Jerusalem is also broken down, and its gates are burned with fire."

⁴ So it was, when I heard these words, that I sat down and wept, and mourned for many days; I was fasting and praying before the God of heaven.

⁵ And I said: "I pray, LORD God of heaven, O great and awesome God, You who keep Your covenant and mercy with those who love You and observe Your commandments, ⁶ please let Your ear be attentive and Your eyes open, that You may hear the prayer of Your servant which I pray before You now, day and night, for the children of Israel Your servants, and confess the sins of the children of Israel which we have sinned against You. Both my father's house and I have sinned. ⁷ We have acted very corruptly against You, and have not kept the commandments, the statutes, nor the ordinances which You commanded Your servant Moses. ⁸ Remember, I pray, the word that You commanded Your servant Moses, saying, 'If you are unfaithful, I will scatter you among the nations; ⁹ but if you return to Me, and keep My commandments and do them, though some of you were cast out to the farthest part of the heavens, yet I will gather them from there, and bring them to the place which I have chosen as a dwelling for My name.' ¹⁰ Now these are Your servants and Your people, whom You have redeemed by Your great power, and by Your strong hand. ¹¹ O Lord, I pray, please let Your ear be attentive to the prayer of Your servant, and to the prayer of Your servants who desire to fear Your name; and let Your servant prosper this day, I pray, and grant him mercy in the sight of this man."

For I was the king's cupbearer.

EXPLORATION

1. How did Nehemiah, who was living in Persia, learn about the condition of the exiles?

_____

_____

_____

2. What was Nehemiah's first response when he heard the news?

3. What does Nehemiah's prayer reveal about his view of himself and of God?

4. Why did Nehemiah "remind" God of the promises that he had made to Moses?

5. How do you think prayer prepared Nehemiah to lead his people?

6. Why would Nehemiah's position have been an asset in improving the situation?

_____

_____

_____

_____

INSPIRATION

Nehemiah 1 is a blend of prayer and action. All who lead must place a high priority on prayer. Why is prayer so important? Here are four short reasons.

First, *prayer makes us wait.* We cannot pray and act at the same time. We have to wait to act until we finish praying. Prayer forces us to leave the situation with God; it makes us wait.

Second, *prayer clears our vision.* Southern California often has an overhanging weather problem in the mornings because of its coastal location until the sun "burns through" the morning fog. Prayer does that. When you first face a situation, is it foggy? Prayer will "burn through." Your vision will clear so you can see through God's eyes.

Third, *prayer quiets our heart.* We cannot worry and pray at the same time. We are doing one or the other. Prayer makes us quiet. It replaces anxiety with a calm spirit. Knees don't knock when we kneel on them!

Fourth, *prayer activates our faith.* After praying, we are more prone to trust God. And how petty and negative and critical we can be when we don't pray! Prayer sets faith on fire.

Don't just fill the margins in your Bible with words and thoughts about ways a leader prays. Do it! Don't just stop with just a sterile theology of prayer. Pray! Prayer was the first major step Nehemiah took in his journey to effective leadership. . . .

The Lord is the Specialist we need for those uncrossable and impossible experiences. He delights in accomplishing what we cannot pull off. But he awaits our cry. He listens for our requests. Nehemiah was quick to call for help. His favorite position when faced with problems was the kneeling position. (From *Hand Me Another Brick* by Charles Swindoll.)

REACTION

7. In what ways does the first chapter of Nehemiah represent "prayer and action"?

---

8. How does prayer clear our vision and cause us to give control of the situation to God?

---

9. How does prayer quiet our hearts and activate our faith?

---

10. If God knows all your fears, desires, and needs, why does he want you to pray about them?

---

11. In what ways has prayer changed your attitude toward a difficult situation you were facing?

_____

_____

_____

12. What ingredients of Nehemiah's prayer do you want to add to your prayer life?

_____

_____

_____

LIFE LESSONS

Passionate prayer is generally prompted by a person's passion to change a situation. In Nehemiah's case, his prayers were birthed out of the sorrow he felt for the condition of his people—and he passionately interceded on their behalf. When presented with a painful situation, there are always two roads we can take. We can become bitter, give in to feelings of helplessness, or even blame God for the circumstances. Or we can choose to believe that God is in control, put the problem in his hands, and continue to trust that he is working for our good. Nehemiah chose the latter option—and then became an _active_ participant in doing God's will.

DEVOTION

Father, we are prone to worry and to complain about our problems. We struggle to solve things on our own instead of depending on you. Forgive us, Father, for living as though we don't need you. Teach us to turn to you first, to face every challenge in your strength, and to give you praise for what you accomplish through us.

JOURNALING

For what task or situation in your life do you need to seek God's guidance and help?

FOR FURTHER READING

To complete the books of Ezra and Nehemiah during this twelve-part study, read Nehemiah 1:1–11. For more Bible passages on crying out to God in prayer, read Exodus 3:7–10; 1 Samuel 7:7–9; Psalm 6:6–10; 34:15–18; Matthew 14:28–31; Mark 4:36–41; Ephesians 6:18–20; and 1 Peter 3:10–12.

CONFIDENCE IN GOD

*I answered the king, "If it pleases the king and
if your servant has found favor in his sight,
let him send me to the city in Judah where my
ancestors are buried so that I can rebuild it."*
NEHEMIAH 2:5

REFLECTION

Think of a time when you had to do something outside your comfort zone in order to achieve a goal. What was the situation? What steps did you have to take?

_____

_____

_____

_____

SITUATION

In Nehemiah's day, it was a common practice for the Persian king's subjects to appear happy and content when in his presence, as this demonstrated the king was being a wise and good ruler. To appear unhappy could actually bring down the king's wrath (see Esther 4:2), so it for good reason Nehemiah is "very much afraid" (Nehemiah 1:2) when the king notices one day that his cupbearer is looking downcast. However, Nehemiah quickly seizes the opportunity to explain the plight of his people—and confidently ask for the king's help in the matter.

OBSERVATION

Read Nehemiah 2:1–20 from the New International
Version or the New King James Version.

NEW INTERNATIONAL VERSION

[1] In the month of Nisan in the twentieth year of King Artaxerxes, when wine was brought for him, I took the wine and gave it to the king. I had not been sad in his presence before, [2] so the king asked me, "Why does

your face look so sad when you are not ill? This can be nothing but sadness of heart."

I was very much afraid, ³ but I said to the king, "May the king live forever! Why should my face not look sad when the city where my ancestors are buried lies in ruins, and its gates have been destroyed by fire?"

⁴ The king said to me, "What is it you want?"

Then I prayed to the God of heaven, ⁵ and I answered the king, "If it pleases the king and if your servant has found favor in his sight, let him send me to the city in Judah where my ancestors are buried so that I can rebuild it."

⁶ Then the king, with the queen sitting beside him, asked me, "How long will your journey take, and when will you get back?" It pleased the king to send me; so I set a time.

⁷ I also said to him, "If it pleases the king, may I have letters to the governors of Trans-Euphrates, so that they will provide me safe-conduct until I arrive in Judah? ⁸ And may I have a letter to Asaph, keeper of the royal park, so he will give me timber to make beams for the gates of the citadel by the temple and for the city wall and for the residence I will occupy?" And because the gracious hand of my God was on me, the king granted my requests. ⁹ So I went to the governors of Trans-Euphrates and gave them the king's letters. The king had also sent army officers and cavalry with me.

¹⁰ When Sanballat the Horonite and Tobiah the Ammonite official heard about this, they were very much disturbed that someone had come to promote the welfare of the Israelites.

¹¹ I went to Jerusalem, and after staying there three days ¹² I set out during the night with a few others. I had not told anyone what my God had put in my heart to do for Jerusalem. There were no mounts with me except the one I was riding on.

¹³ By night I went out through the Valley Gate toward the Jackal Well and the Dung Gate, examining the walls of Jerusalem, which had been broken down, and its gates, which had been destroyed by fire. ¹⁴ Then I moved on toward the Fountain Gate and the King's Pool, but there was not enough room for my mount to get through; ¹⁵ so I went up the

valley by night, examining the wall. Finally, I turned back and reentered through the Valley Gate. [16] The officials did not know where I had gone or what I was doing, because as yet I had said nothing to the Jews or the priests or nobles or officials or any others who would be doing the work.

[17] Then I said to them, "You see the trouble we are in: Jerusalem lies in ruins, and its gates have been burned with fire. Come, let us rebuild the wall of Jerusalem, and we will no longer be in disgrace." [18] I also told them about the gracious hand of my God on me and what the king had said to me.

They replied, "Let us start rebuilding." So they began this good work.

[19] But when Sanballat the Horonite, Tobiah the Ammonite official and Geshem the Arab heard about it, they mocked and ridiculed us. "What is this you are doing?" they asked. "Are you rebelling against the king?"

[20] I answered them by saying, "The God of heaven will give us success. We his servants will start rebuilding, but as for you, you have no share in Jerusalem or any claim or historic right to it."

New King James Version

[1] And it came to pass in the month of Nisan, in the twentieth year of King Artaxerxes, when wine was before him, that I took the wine and gave it to the king. Now I had never been sad in his presence before. [2] Therefore the king said to me, "Why is your face sad, since you are not sick? This is nothing but sorrow of heart."

So I became dreadfully afraid, [3] and said to the king, "May the king live forever! Why should my face not be sad, when the city, the place of my fathers' tombs, lies waste, and its gates are burned with fire?"

[4] Then the king said to me, "What do you request?"

So I prayed to the God of heaven. [5] And I said to the king, "If it pleases the king, and if your servant has found favor in your sight, I ask that you send me to Judah, to the city of my fathers' tombs, that I may rebuild it."

[6] Then the king said to me (the queen also sitting beside him), "How long will your journey be? And when will you return?" So it pleased the king to send me; and I set him a time.

[7] Furthermore I said to the king, "If it pleases the king, let letters be given to me for the governors of the region beyond the River, that they must permit me to pass through till I come to Judah, [8] and a letter to Asaph the keeper of the king's forest, that he must give me timber to make beams for the gates of the citadel which pertains to the temple, for the city wall, and for the house that I will occupy." And the king granted them to me according to the good hand of my God upon me.

[9] Then I went to the governors in the region beyond the River, and gave them the king's letters. Now the king had sent captains of the army and horsemen with me. [10] When Sanballat the Horonite and Tobiah the Ammonite official heard of it, they were deeply disturbed that a man had come to seek the well-being of the children of Israel.

[11] So I came to Jerusalem and was there three days. [12] Then I arose in the night, I and a few men with me; I told no one what my God had put in my heart to do at Jerusalem; nor was there any animal with me, except the one on which I rode. [13] And I went out by night through the Valley Gate to the Serpent Well and the Refuse Gate, and viewed the walls of Jerusalem which were broken down and its gates which were burned with fire. [14] Then I went on to the Fountain Gate and to the King's Pool, but there was no room for the animal under me to pass. [15] So I went up in the night by the valley, and viewed the wall; then I turned back and entered by the Valley Gate, and so returned. [16] And the officials did not know where I had gone or what I had done; I had not yet told the Jews, the priests, the nobles, the officials, or the others who did the work.

[17] Then I said to them, "You see the distress that we are in, how Jerusalem lies waste, and its gates are burned with fire. Come and let us build the wall of Jerusalem, that we may no longer be a reproach." [18] And I told them of the hand of my God which had been good upon me, and also of the king's words that he had spoken to me.

So they said, "Let us rise up and build." Then they set their hands to this good work.

[19] But when Sanballat the Horonite, Tobiah the Ammonite official, and Geshem the Arab heard of it, they laughed at us and despised us,

and said, "What is this thing that you are doing? Will you rebel against the king?"

²⁰ So I answered them, and said to them, "The God of heaven Himself will prosper us; therefore we His servants will arise and build, but you have no heritage or right or memorial in Jerusalem."

EXPLORATION

1. Why was Nehemiah "very much afraid" (verse 2) when the king asked why he was sad?

_____

_____

_____

_____

_____

2. Why did it take courage for Nehemiah to speak to the king on behalf of the exiles?

_____

_____

_____

_____

_____

3. How did Nehemiah demonstrate he sought God throughout this exchange with the king?

_____

_____

_____

_____

4. What was Nehemiah's bold request to the king? How did the king respond?

_____

_____

_____

_____

5. Why did Nehemiah go out at night in secret to survey the damage to Jerusalem's walls?

_____

_____

_____

_____

6. How did Nehemiah respond when his enemies said he was rebelling against the Persian king?

_____

_____

_____

INSPIRATION

When Martin Luther's coworker became ill, the reformer prayed boldly for healing. "I besought the Almighty with great vigor," he wrote. "I attacked him with his own weapons, quoting from Scripture all the promises I could remember, that prayers should be granted, and said that he must grant my prayer, if I was henceforth to put faith in his promises."

On another occasion his good friend Frederick Myconius was sick. Luther wrote to him: "I command thee in the name of God to live because

I still have need of thee in the work of reforming the church. . . . The Lord will never let me hear that thou art dead, but will permit thee to survive me. For this I am praying, this is my will, and may my will be done, because I seek only to glorify the name of God."

As John Wesley was crossing the Atlantic Ocean, contrary winds came up. He was reading in his cabin when he became aware of some confusion on board. When he learned that the winds were knocking the ship off course, he responded in prayer.

Adam Clarke, a colleague, heard the prayer and recorded it: "Almighty and everlasting God, thou hast sway everywhere, and all things serve the purpose of thy will, thou holdest the winds in thy fists and sittest upon the water floods, and reignest a king for ever. Command these winds and these waves that they obey thee, and take us speedily and safely to the haven whither we would go."

Wesley stood up from his knees, took up his book, and continued to read. Dr. Clarke went on deck, where he found calm winds and the ship on course. But Wesley made no remark about the answered prayer. Clarke wrote, "So fully did he expect to be heard that he took it for granted that he was heard."

How bold are your prayers?

Boldness in prayer is an uncomfortable thought for many. We think of speaking softly to God, humbling ourselves before God, or having a chat with God . . . but agonizing before God? Storming heaven with prayers? Pounding on the door of the Most High? Wrestling with God? Isn't such prayer irreverent? Presumptuous?

It would be had God not invited us to pray as such. "Let us then approach God's throne of grace with confidence, so that we may receive mercy and find grace to help us in our time of need" (Hebrews 4:16). . . . Our relationship with God is exactly that: a relationship. His invitation is clear and simple: "Come and talk with me, O my people" (Psalm 27:8 TLB). And our response? "Lord, I am coming" (verse 8 TLB). We abide with him, and he abides with us. He grants wisdom as we need it. (From *Glory Days* by Max Lucado.)

REACTION

7. How do you respond to the idea that God wants you to be bold in your prayers and approach his throne with confidence?

_____

_____

_____

_____

_____

8. When is the last time that you "stormed heaven" with a request to God?

_____

_____

_____

_____

9. What is a problem you are facing right now that you need to pray about with confidence?

_____

_____

_____

_____

10. What are some bold requests you have made in the past that you have seen God answer?

_____

_____

_____

_____

11. In what ways have the testimonies of others about prayer helped you trust God?

_____

_____

_____

_____

12. What are some steps you can take today to pray with more confidence?

_____

_____

_____

LIFE LESSONS

God delights in surprising us. When Nehemiah stood up for his people and made a bold request to the king on their behalf—*surprise!*—God moved the king's heart to grant the request and provide Nehemiah with the resources he would need to rebuild Jerusalem's walls. God will surprise us as well when we make bold requests to him. As Jesus promised, "If you have faith as small as a mustard seed, you can say to this mountain, 'Move from here to there,' and it will move" (Matthew 17:20). Sadly, all too often we "do not have" because we "do not ask God" (James 4:2). If we want to see God surprise us with answers to our prayers, we have to believe there is nothing too great for him to do—and then approach his throne with confidence.

DEVOTION

Father, you are our fortress, our refuge, and our safe harbor. Teach us to run to you whenever we feel overwhelmed with a problem and trust that you can solve it. Help us to be bold and confident in our requests—knowing there is nothing too great for you to handle.

JOURNALING

What is a specific need in another person's life that you will confidently pray about today?

FOR FURTHER READING

To complete the books of Ezra and Nehemiah during this twelve-part study, read Nehemiah 2:1–3:16. For more Bible passages on praying boldly, read Exodus 32:9–14; 1 Kings 18:36–38; Acts 28:30–31; Ephesians 6:18–20; Hebrews 4:14–16; James 5:13–16; and 1 John 3:19–22.

PERSEVERING IN TRIALS

"Do not be afraid of them. Remember the Lord, great and awesome, and fight for your brethren, your sons, your daughters, your wives, and your houses."
NEHEMIAH 4:14 NKJV

REFLECTION

Think of a time you felt like giving up on a project. What motivated you to stick with it?

_____

_____

_____

_____

_____

SITUATION

It isn't long after Nehemiah arrives in Jerusalem to survey the damage to the walls and begin work on the repairs that he is beset by a host of enemies who want to derail his efforts. Two men, named Sanballat (the governor of Samaria) and Tobiah (the governor of the region east of the Jordan River), soon join forces to harass the people in their work. Nehemiah refuses to allow them to discourage him, and when these enemies see the wall is half finished, they take it upon themselves to mobilize an armed aggression against the workers. Staying on task requires Nehemiah to persevere in these trials—and the same is required of us when facing our enemy.

OBSERVATION

*Read Nehemiah 4:1–23 from the New International
Version or the New King James Version.*

NEW INTERNATIONAL VERSION

¹ When Sanballat heard that we were rebuilding the wall, he became angry and was greatly incensed. He ridiculed the Jews, ² and in the presence of his associates and the army of Samaria, he said, "What are those

feeble Jews doing? Will they restore their wall? Will they offer sacrifices? Will they finish in a day? Can they bring the stones back to life from those heaps of rubble—burned as they are?"

³ Tobiah the Ammonite, who was at his side, said, "What they are building—even a fox climbing up on it would break down their wall of stones!"

⁴ Hear us, our God, for we are despised. Turn their insults back on their own heads. Give them over as plunder in a land of captivity. ⁵ Do not cover up their guilt or blot out their sins from your sight, for they have thrown insults in the face of the builders.

⁶ So we rebuilt the wall till all of it reached half its height, for the people worked with all their heart.

⁷ But when Sanballat, Tobiah, the Arabs, the Ammonites and the people of Ashdod heard that the repairs to Jerusalem's walls had gone ahead and that the gaps were being closed, they were very angry. ⁸ They all plotted together to come and fight against Jerusalem and stir up trouble against it. ⁹ But we prayed to our God and posted a guard day and night to meet this threat.

¹⁰ Meanwhile, the people in Judah said, "The strength of the laborers is giving out, and there is so much rubble that we cannot rebuild the wall."

¹¹ Also our enemies said, "Before they know it or see us, we will be right there among them and will kill them and put an end to the work."

¹² Then the Jews who lived near them came and told us ten times over, "Wherever you turn, they will attack us."

¹³ Therefore I stationed some of the people behind the lowest points of the wall at the exposed places, posting them by families, with their swords, spears and bows. ¹⁴ After I looked things over, I stood up and said to the nobles, the officials and the rest of the people, "Don't be afraid of them. Remember the Lord, who is great and awesome, and fight for your families, your sons and your daughters, your wives and your homes."

¹⁵ When our enemies heard that we were aware of their plot and that God had frustrated it, we all returned to the wall, each to our own work.

¹⁶ From that day on, half of my men did the work, while the other half were equipped with spears, shields, bows and armor. The officers posted

themselves behind all the people of Judah ¹⁷ who were building the wall. Those who carried materials did their work with one hand and held a weapon in the other, ¹⁸ and each of the builders wore his sword at his side as he worked. But the man who sounded the trumpet stayed with me.

¹⁹ Then I said to the nobles, the officials and the rest of the people, "The work is extensive and spread out, and we are widely separated from each other along the wall. ²⁰ Wherever you hear the sound of the trumpet, join us there. Our God will fight for us!"

²¹ So we continued the work with half the men holding spears, from the first light of dawn till the stars came out. ²² At that time I also said to the people, "Have every man and his helper stay inside Jerusalem at night, so they can serve us as guards by night and as workers by day." ²³ Neither I nor my brothers nor my men nor the guards with me took off our clothes; each had his weapon, even when he went for water.

NEW KING JAMES VERSION

¹ But it so happened, when Sanballat heard that we were rebuilding the wall, that he was furious and very indignant, and mocked the Jews. ² And he spoke before his brethren and the army of Samaria, and said, "What are these feeble Jews doing? Will they fortify themselves? Will they offer sacrifices? Will they complete it in a day? Will they revive the stones from the heaps of rubbish—stones that are burned?"

³ Now Tobiah the Ammonite was beside him, and he said, "Whatever they build, if even a fox goes up on it, he will break down their stone wall."

⁴ Hear, O our God, for we are despised; turn their reproach on their own heads, and give them as plunder to a land of captivity! ⁵ Do not cover their iniquity, and do not let their sin be blotted out from before You; for they have provoked You to anger before the builders.

⁶ So we built the wall, and the entire wall was joined together up to half its height, for the people had a mind to work.

⁷ Now it happened, when Sanballat, Tobiah, the Arabs, the Ammonites, and the Ashdodites heard that the walls of Jerusalem were being restored and the gaps were beginning to be closed, that they became very angry,

[8] and all of them conspired together to come and attack Jerusalem and create confusion. [9] Nevertheless we made our prayer to our God, and because of them we set a watch against them day and night.

[10] Then Judah said, "The strength of the laborers is failing, and there is so much rubbish that we are not able to build the wall."

[11] And our adversaries said, "They will neither know nor see anything, till we come into their midst and kill them and cause the work to cease."

[12] So it was, when the Jews who dwelt near them came, that they told us ten times, "From whatever place you turn, they will be upon us."

[13] Therefore I positioned men behind the lower parts of the wall, at the openings; and I set the people according to their families, with their swords, their spears, and their bows. [14] And I looked, and arose and said to the nobles, to the leaders, and to the rest of the people, "Do not be afraid of them. Remember the Lord, great and awesome, and fight for your brethren, your sons, your daughters, your wives, and your houses."

[15] And it happened, when our enemies heard that it was known to us, and that God had brought their plot to nothing, that all of us returned to the wall, everyone to his work. [16] So it was, from that time on, that half of my servants worked at construction, while the other half held the spears, the shields, the bows, and wore armor; and the leaders were behind all the house of Judah. [17] Those who built on the wall, and those who carried burdens, loaded themselves so that with one hand they worked at construction, and with the other held a weapon. [18] Every one of the builders had his sword girded at his side as he built. And the one who sounded the trumpet was beside me.

[19] Then I said to the nobles, the rulers, and the rest of the people, "The work is great and extensive, and we are separated far from one another on the wall. [20] Wherever you hear the sound of the trumpet, rally to us there. Our God will fight for us."

[21] So we labored in the work, and half of the men held the spears from daybreak until the stars appeared. [22] At the same time I also said to the people, "Let each man and his servant stay at night in Jerusalem, that

they may be our guard by night and a working party by day." [23] So neither I, my brethren, my servants, nor the men of the guard who followed me took off our clothes, except that everyone took them off for washing.

EXPLORATION

1. How did Sanballat and Tobiah initially try to discourage the peoples' rebuilding effort?

_____

_____

_____

_____

2. How did Nehemiah respond to their ridicule (see verses 4–5)?

_____

_____

_____

3. How did Nehemiah respond when their enemies banded to together to fight them?

_____

_____

_____

4. What other internal problems did Nehemiah face in building the wall (see verse 10)?

_____

_____

_____

5. What was the wisdom of the plan Nehemiah devised to protect the people while still accomplishing the task of rebuilding the wall?

_____

_____

_____

6. What leadership traits did Nehemiah possess that enabled his people to persevere?

_____

_____

_____

INSPIRATION

Have you ever known a time when you thought you would die if the Lord did not give you his touch? A time when no friend could comfort you? When you could see no way out? When your circumstances gave new meaning to the word bleak?

A man named Bart decided to ask God to shape his character. He surrendered his own will to the will of God. At the time, Bart's business floundered on the verge of failure. "Should I throw in the towel, or keep trying to hang on?" Bart wondered.

God replied, "You need to persevere." After we have done the will of God, then we will receive our reward. God's will is for us to demonstrate to a hurting world how wonderfully His power can work within the person who perseveres.

Certainly, there are days when we feel like we will die, or maybe even wished we could, but we keep going. Why? Why do we keep going? Because _when_ we have done the will of God, we _will_ receive what He has promised.

Will persevering guarantee we will succeed in the worldly sense of success? Is that what He has promised? Does it mean we will not go out of business if we hang on? No, but we can state emphatically that if we don't persevere we will not succeed in any sense. Not persevering guarantees we will fail.

What exactly is it, then, that He has promised? Jesus said, "Whoever does God's will is my brother and sister and mother" (Mark 3:35). When you have persevered, you become transformed into part of the family of Christ. You become His friend, and He prays for you in the presence of the Father.

Beyond succeeding in a worldly sense, though, God wants our character to succeed more than our circumstances succeed. He will adjust our circumstances in such a way that our character eventually succeeds, for that is His highest aim, His will. (From *Walking with Christ in the Details of Life* by Patrick Morley.)

REACTION

7. When is a time in your life that you had to persevere in a situation?

_____

_____

_____

8. What rewards did you realize as a result of your perseverance?

_____

_____

_____

9. How can persevering in a trial—even if you don't receive the outcome you want—serve to strengthen your relationship with Christ?

_____

_____

_____

10. How can persevering demonstrate to the world your complete trust in God?

11. How can you encourage a friend today who feels like giving up?

12. Which of Nehemiah's character traits would you most like to cultivate in your own life?

LIFE LESSONS

Even though Nehemiah knew he was following God's will when he instructed the people to rebuild the walls around Jerusalem, he still experienced opposition and ridicule at the hands of his enemies. All too often we tend to believe that if we are doing what God has instructed, we should have an easy and pain-free time of it. But the reality is that opposition is a given in the Christian life. As Paul stated frankly, "For it has been granted to you on behalf of Christ not only to believe in him, but *also to suffer for him*" (Philippians 1:29, emphasis added). God grants us faith, but he also grants us suffering. Why? Because, as James wrote, "the testing of your faith produces perseverance . . . so that you may be mature and complete" (James 1:3–4).

DEVOTION

Father, we know you allow us to experience troubles because you want to strengthen our character. We ask you to help us view our problems as opportunities to learn and grow. In the face of opposition, help us to stand firm. May our lives be a model of faithfulness to you.

JOURNALING

What is a situation in your life right now that is helping you to develop perseverance?

_____

_____

_____

_____

_____

_____

_____

_____

_____

_____

_____

FOR FURTHER READING

To complete the books of Ezra and Nehemiah during this twelve-part study, read Nehemiah 3:17–4:23. For more Bible passages on perseverance, read 1 Chronicles 16:8–11; Psalm 138:1–3; Luke 15:11–15; 1 Corinthians 9:24–27; Galatians 6:8–10; 1 Timothy 4:15–16; Hebrews 12:1–3; James 5:10–11; and Revelation 2:2–3.

HELP FOR THE HURTING

"As far as possible, we have bought back our fellow Jews who were sold to the Gentiles. Now you are selling your own people, only for them to be sold back to us!"
NEHEMIAH 5:8

REFLECTION

Who is someone in your life who reached out to you when you were in need? What did that person's support mean to you at that time?

_____

_____

_____

_____

SITUATION

Nehemiah not only had to deal with outside threats from enemies like Sanballat and Tobiah but also with internal strife at the hands of his own people. Due to the hectic work schedule on the wall, many of the people did not have the time or the energy to attend to their own personal matters. As a result, some of the people were experiencing financial difficulties and even going hungry. When Nehemiah learns these workers are being exploited by the wealthy officials and nobles in the region, he sets out to address the problem and provide help to the hurting.

OBSERVATION

Read Nehemiah 5:1–13 from the New International Version or the New King James Version.

NEW INTERNATIONAL VERSION
[1] Now the men and their wives raised a great outcry against their fellow Jews. [2] Some were saying, "We and our sons and daughters are numerous; in order for us to eat and stay alive, we must get grain."

[3] Others were saying, "We are mortgaging our fields, our vineyards and our homes to get grain during the famine."

⁴ Still others were saying, "We have had to borrow money to pay the king's tax on our fields and vineyards. ⁵ Although we are of the same flesh and blood as our fellow Jews and though our children are as good as theirs, yet we have to subject our sons and daughters to slavery. Some of our daughters have already been enslaved, but we are powerless, because our fields and our vineyards belong to others."

⁶ When I heard their outcry and these charges, I was very angry. ⁷ I pondered them in my mind and then accused the nobles and officials. I told them, "You are charging your own people interest!" So I called together a large meeting to deal with them ⁸ and said: "As far as possible, we have bought back our fellow Jews who were sold to the Gentiles. Now you are selling your own people, only for them to be sold back to us!" They kept quiet, because they could find nothing to say.

⁹ So I continued, "What you are doing is not right. Shouldn't you walk in the fear of our God to avoid the reproach of our Gentile enemies? ¹⁰ I and my brothers and my men are also lending the people money and grain. But let us stop charging interest! ¹¹ Give back to them immediately their fields, vineyards, olive groves and houses, and also the interest you are charging them—one percent of the money, grain, new wine and olive oil."

¹² "We will give it back," they said. "And we will not demand anything more from them. We will do as you say."

Then I summoned the priests and made the nobles and officials take an oath to do what they had promised. ¹³ I also shook out the folds of my robe and said, "In this way may God shake out of their house and possessions anyone who does not keep this promise. So may such a person be shaken out and emptied!"

At this the whole assembly said, "Amen," and praised the LORD. And the people did as they had promised.

NEW KING JAMES VERSION

¹ And there was a great outcry of the people and their wives against their Jewish brethren. ² For there were those who said, "We, our sons, and our daughters are many; therefore let us get grain, that we may eat and live."

³ There were also some who said, "We have mortgaged our lands and vineyards and houses, that we might buy grain because of the famine."

⁴ There were also those who said, "We have borrowed money for the king's tax on our lands and vineyards. ⁵ Yet now our flesh is as the flesh of our brethren, our children as their children; and indeed we are forcing our sons and our daughters to be slaves, and some of our daughters have been brought into slavery. It is not in our power to redeem them, for other men have our lands and vineyards."

⁶ And I became very angry when I heard their outcry and these words. ⁷ After serious thought, I rebuked the nobles and rulers, and said to them, "Each of you is exacting usury from his brother." So I called a great assembly against them. ⁸ And I said to them, "According to our ability we have redeemed our Jewish brethren who were sold to the nations. Now indeed, will you even sell your brethren? Or should they be sold to us?"

Then they were silenced and found nothing to say. ⁹ Then I said, "What you are doing is not good. Should you not walk in the fear of our God because of the reproach of the nations, our enemies? ¹⁰ I also, with my brethren and my servants, am lending them money and grain. Please, let us stop this usury! ¹¹ Restore now to them, even this day, their lands, their vineyards, their olive groves, and their houses, also a hundredth of the money and the grain, the new wine and the oil, that you have charged them."

¹² So they said, "We will restore it, and will require nothing from them; we will do as you say."

Then I called the priests, and required an oath from them that they would do according to this promise. ¹³ Then I shook out the fold of my garment and said, "So may God shake out each man from his house, and from his property, who does not perform this promise. Even thus may he be shaken out and emptied."

And all the assembly said, "Amen!" and praised the LORD. Then the people did according to this promise.

EXPLORATION

1. What was the complaint some of the exiles raised against their fellow countrymen?

2. How did Nehemiah respond when he first heard the accusations?

3. How did Nehemiah come to the defense of those who were suffering?

4. What did Nehemiah mean when he said the wealthier citizens were "selling" their own people (see verse 8)?

5. What did Nehemiah say these citizens needed to immediately do to remedy the problem?

6. According to Nehemiah, people who fear God should treat the poor with kindness and deference. How does that apply to believers in today's world?

_____

_____

_____

INSPIRATION

May I ask you to look at your hand for a moment? Look at the back, then the palm. Reacquaint yourself with your fingers. Run a thumb over your knuckles.

What if someone were to film a documentary on your hands? What if a producer were to tell your story based on the life of your hands? What would we see? As with all of us, the film would begin with an infant's fist, then a close-up of a tiny hand wrapped around Mommy's finger. Then what? Holding on to a chair as you learned to walk? Handling a spoon as you learned to eat?

We aren't too long into the feature before we see your hand being affectionate, stroking Daddy's face or petting a puppy. Nor is it too long before we see your hand acting aggressively: pushing big brother or yanking back a toy. All of us learned early that the hand is suited for more than survival—it's a tool of emotional expression. The same hand can help or hurt, extend or clench, lift someone up or shove someone down.

Were you to show the documentary to your friends, you'd be proud of certain moments: your hand extending with a gift, placing a ring on another's finger, doctoring a wound, preparing a meal, or folding in prayer. And then there are other scenes. Shots of accusing fingers, abusive fists. Hands taking more often than giving, demanding instead of offering, wounding rather than loving.

Oh, the power of our hands. Leave them unmanaged and they become weapons: clawing for power, strangling for survival, seducing for pleasure. But manage them and our hands become instruments of grace—not just tools in the hands of God, but *God's very hands*. Surrender them and these five-fingered appendages become the hands of heaven.

That's what Jesus did. Our Savior completely surrendered his hands to God. The documentary of his hands has no scenes of greedy grabbing or unfounded finger-pointing. It does, however, have one scene after another of people longing for his compassionate touch: parents carrying their children, the poor bringing their fears, the sinful shouldering their sorrow. And each who came was touched. And each one touched was changed. (From *Just Like Jesus* by Max Lucado.)

REACTION

7. How has God used your "hands" as an instrument of his grace?

_____

_____

_____

_____

8. What are some ways that Jesus completely surrendered his hands to God?

_____

_____

_____

_____

9. How does the story of the suffering exiles in Nehemiah show that God cares for the hurting?

_____

_____

_____

10. How has God met a physical, emotional, or financial need in your life?

---

11. What responsibility do you have to help the poor and oppressed?

---

12. Who is one hurting person you can reach with God's love this week?

LIFE LESSONS

While God does "not show favoritism" (Romans 2:11), he has a special place in his heart for the poor. "He defends the cause of the fatherless and the widow, and loves the foreigner residing among you, giving them food and clothing" (Deuteronomy 10:18). The writer or Proverbs 14:31 stated, "Whoever oppresses the poor shows contempt for their Maker, but whoever is kind to the needy honors God," and James later wrote, "Religion that God our Father accepts as pure and faultless is this: to look after orphans and widows in their distress" (James 1:27). God loves the poor, but he does not want them to stay that way. Our calling as believers in Christ, just as in Nehemiah's day, is to help the hurting and seek to alleviate the oppression they are facing.

DEVOTION

Father, we're grateful you are concerned with our needs. You comfort the hurting, provide for the poor, and deliver the oppressed. Help us today to be your "hands and feet" in the world so we may be your instruments in alleviating the suffering of others. Thank you, Lord.

JOURNALING

What are some ways this week that you can help another person in need?

FOR FURTHER READING

To complete the books of Ezra and Nehemiah during this twelve-part study, read Nehemiah 5:1–7:73. For more Bible passages on God's care for the hurting, read Deuteronomy 27:17–19; Psalm 68:4–6; Isaiah 1:16–17; Luke 14:12–14; Acts 4:32–35; 1 Timothy 5:1–8; Hebrews 13:1–3; and James 1:22–27.

LOVE AND FAITHFULNESS

"They refused to obey . . . they hardened their necks. . . .
But You are God, ready to pardon, gracious and merciful, slow
to anger, abundant in kindness, and did not forsake them."
NEHEMIAH 9:17 NKJV

REFLECTION

What are some ways God has demonstrated his steadfast faithfulness to you?

_____

_____

_____

_____

SITUATION

In spite of all the external and internal struggles, Nehemiah is able to complete the wall around Jerusalem in just fifty-two days. He assigns some of the residents to continue protecting the city, puts his brother Hanani in charge, and conducts a census or "registration" of the people. When this is complete, Nehemiah calls Ezra to read "the Book of the Law" (Nehemiah 8:1) at a public gathering. Many of the people weep when they hear the words, as they are realizing just how they have failed to honor God and live by his commands. Together, the people confess their sin and make a binding agreement to love the Lord and always be faithful to him.

OBSERVATION

Read Nehemiah 9:5–21 from the New International Version or the New King James Version.

NEW INTERNATIONAL VERSION

5 And the Levites—Jeshua, Kadmiel, Bani, Hashabneiah, Sherebiah, Hodiah, Shebaniah and Pethahiah—said: "Stand up and praise the LORD your God, who is from everlasting to everlasting."

"Blessed be your glorious name, and may it be exalted above all blessing and praise. ⁶ You alone are the LORD. You made the heavens, even the highest heavens, and all their starry host, the earth and all that is on it, the seas and all that is in them. You give life to everything, and the multitudes of heaven worship you.

⁷ "You are the LORD God, who chose Abram and brought him out of Ur of the Chaldeans and named him Abraham. ⁸ You found his heart faithful to you, and you made a covenant with him to give to his descendants the land of the Canaanites, Hittites, Amorites, Perizzites, Jebusites and Girgashites. You have kept your promise because you are righteous.

⁹ "You saw the suffering of our ancestors in Egypt; you heard their cry at the Red Sea. ¹⁰ You sent signs and wonders against Pharaoh, against all his officials and all the people of his land, for you knew how arrogantly the Egyptians treated them. You made a name for yourself, which remains to this day. ¹¹ You divided the sea before them, so that they passed through it on dry ground, but you hurled their pursuers into the depths, like a stone into mighty waters. ¹² By day you led them with a pillar of cloud, and by night with a pillar of fire to give them light on the way they were to take.

¹³ "You came down on Mount Sinai; you spoke to them from heaven. You gave them regulations and laws that are just and right, and decrees and commands that are good. ¹⁴ You made known to them your holy Sabbath and gave them commands, decrees and laws through your servant Moses. ¹⁵ In their hunger you gave them bread from heaven and in their thirst you brought them water from the rock; you told them to go in and take possession of the land you had sworn with uplifted hand to give them.

¹⁶ "But they, our ancestors, became arrogant and stiff-necked, and they did not obey your commands. ¹⁷ They refused to listen and failed to remember the miracles you performed among them. They became stiff-necked and in their rebellion appointed a leader in order to return to their slavery. But you are a forgiving God, gracious

and compassionate, slow to anger and abounding in love. Therefore you did not desert them, [18] even when they cast for themselves an image of a calf and said, 'This is your god, who brought you up out of Egypt,' or when they committed awful blasphemies.

[19] "Because of your great compassion you did not abandon them in the wilderness. By day the pillar of cloud did not fail to guide them on their path, nor the pillar of fire by night to shine on the way they were to take. [20] You gave your good Spirit to instruct them. You did not withhold your manna from their mouths, and you gave them water for their thirst. [21] For forty years you sustained them in the wilderness; they lacked nothing, their clothes did not wear out nor did their feet become swollen."

NEW KING JAMES VERSION

[5] And the Levites, Jeshua, Kadmiel, Bani, Hashabniah, Sherebiah, Hodijah, Shebaniah, and Pethahiah, said:

"Stand up and bless the LORD your God
Forever and ever!

"Blessed be Your glorious name,
Which is exalted above all blessing and praise!
[6] You alone are the LORD;
You have made heaven,
The heaven of heavens, with all their host,
The earth and everything on it,
The seas and all that is in them,
And You preserve them all.
The host of heaven worships You.

[7] "You are the LORD God,
Who chose Abram,
And brought him out of Ur of the Chaldeans,

And gave him the name Abraham;
[8] You found his heart faithful before You,
And made a covenant with him
To give the land of the Canaanites,
The Hittites, the Amorites,
The Perizzites, the Jebusites,
And the Girgashites—
To give it to his descendants.
You have performed Your words,
For You are righteous.

[9] "You saw the affliction of our fathers in Egypt,
And heard their cry by the Red Sea.
[10] You showed signs and wonders against Pharaoh,
Against all his servants,
And against all the people of his land.
For You knew that they acted proudly against them.
So You made a name for Yourself, as it is this day.
[11] And You divided the sea before them,
So that they went through the midst of the sea on the dry land;
And their persecutors You threw into the deep,
As a stone into the mighty waters.
[12] Moreover You led them by day with a cloudy pillar,
And by night with a pillar of fire,
To give them light on the road
Which they should travel.

[13] "You came down also on Mount Sinai,
And spoke with them from heaven,
And gave them just ordinances and true laws,
Good statutes and commandments.
[14] You made known to them Your holy Sabbath,
And commanded them precepts, statutes and laws,

By the hand of Moses Your servant.
[15] You gave them bread from heaven for their hunger,
And brought them water out of the rock for their thirst,
And told them to go in to possess the land
Which You had sworn to give them.

[16] "But they and our fathers acted proudly,
Hardened their necks,
And did not heed Your commandments.
[17] They refused to obey,
And they were not mindful of Your wonders
That You did among them.
But they hardened their necks,
And in their rebellion
They appointed a leader
To return to their bondage.
But You are God,
Ready to pardon,
Gracious and merciful,
Slow to anger,
Abundant in kindness,
And did not forsake them.

[18] "Even when they made a molded calf for themselves,
And said, 'This is your god
That brought you up out of Egypt,'
And worked great provocations,
[19] Yet in Your manifold mercies
You did not forsake them in the wilderness.
The pillar of the cloud did not depart from them by day,
To lead them on the road;
Nor the pillar of fire by night,
To show them light,

And the way they should go.
[20] You also gave Your good Spirit to instruct them,
And did not withhold Your manna from their mouth,
And gave them water for their thirst.
[21] Forty years You sustained them in the wilderness;
They lacked nothing;
Their clothes did not wear out
And their feet did not swell."

EXPLORATION

1. How had God demonstrated his faithfulness to the Jewish people in the past?

_____

_____

_____

2. How had God demonstrated that he was present with his people?

_____

_____

3. What did God ask of the people in return?

_____

_____

4. Why did the Israelites break their covenant with God after all he had provided for them?

_____

_____

5. How did God demonstrate his faithfulness in spite of the people's rebellion?

_____

_____

_____

6. Why would this summary of God's faithfulness to his people in the past have been beneficial to the Jewish exiles in Nehemiah's day?

_____

_____

_____

INSPIRATION

God is in the thick of things in your world. He has not taken up residence in a distant galaxy. He has not removed himself from history. He has not chosen to seclude himself on a throne in an incandescent castle.

He has drawn near. He has involved himself in the carpools, heartbreaks, and funeral homes of our day. He is as near to us on Monday as on Sunday. In the schoolroom as in the sanctuary. At the coffee break as much as the communion table.

Why? Why did God do it? What was his reason?

Some years ago Denalyn was gone for a couple of days and left me alone with the girls. Though the time was not without the typical children's quarrels and occasional misbehavior, it went fine.

How were the girls?" Denalyn asked when she got home.

"Good. No problem at all."

Jenna overheard my response. "We weren't good, Daddy," she objected. "We fought once; we didn't do what you said once. We weren't good. How can you say we were good?"

Jenna and I had different perceptions of what pleases a father. She thought it depended upon what she did. It didn't. We think the same about God. We think his love rises and falls with our performance. It doesn't. I don't love Jenna for what she does. I love her for whose she is. She is mine.

God loves you for the same reason. He loves you for whose you are; you are his child. It was this love that pursued the Israelites. It was this love that sent the prophets. It was this love that wrapped itself in human flesh and descended the birth canal of Mary. It was this love that walked the hard trails of Galilee and spoke to the hard hearts of the religious. . . .

God comes to your house, steps up to the door, and knocks. But it's up to you to let him in. (From *And the Angels Were Silent* by Max Lucado.)

REACTION

7. How has God demonstrated that he is "in the thick of things" in your world?

8. Why is it important that you serve a God who is ever-present and knows your concerns?

9. What are some common misconceptions people have about how God relates to us?

10. What are the benefits of remembering God's past works in your life?

_____

_____

_____

11. What happens when you ignore or forget what God has done for you in the past?

_____

_____

_____

12. How do you respond to knowing that God will love you and remain faithful to you in spite of how often you fail him?

_____

_____

_____

LIFE LESSONS

The Hebrew word for God's loyal love is *hesed*. It appears twenty-six times in Psalm 136 where this phrase is repeated: "Give thanks to the LORD, for he is good. His love [*hesed*] endures forever." God demonstrated this type of love when he delivered the Israelites from Egypt and made them into a nation. He asked only that they love him in return— but time and again, they rebelled against him. God's love wasn't a fickle emotion or mere words. His love (*hesed*) had great patience, unlimited compassion, and undiluted faithfulness. He relentlessly pursued his people and invited them back into a relationship with him. He does the same today. In fact it was the mission of Jesus, who "came to seek and to save the lost" (Luke 19:10).

DEVOTION

Father, thank you for pursuing us with an everlasting love. Thank you for making us your children and for loving us as your own. We praise you for your faithfulness and trustworthiness. Deepen our understanding of your love and help us to remain faithful to you.

JOURNALING

What are some ways that God has revealed his love and faithfulness to you?

FOR FURTHER READING

To complete the books of Ezra and Nehemiah during this twelve-part study, read Nehemiah 8:1–10:27. For more Bible passages on God's faithfulness, read Exodus 34:5–7; Numbers 23:18–19; Deuteronomy 7:7–9; Psalm 33:4–5; Romans 5:6–8; 1 Corinthians 1:4–9; 2 Thessalonians 3:3–5; and 1 John 1:8–9.

A GENEROUS HEART

*"We also assume responsibility for bringing to
the house of the LORD each year the firstfruits
of our crops and of every fruit tree."*
NEHEMIAH 10:35

REFLECTION

When is a time in your life that you were blessed by the generosity of another person?

_____

_____

_____

_____

_____

_____

SITUATION

The book of Nehemiah concludes the account of the "binding agreement" the people made with God by giving an official list of those who "sealed" or consented to follow it. The rest of the people also vowed to follow the terms of the agreement, promising not to intermarry with foreigners or violate God's laws concerning the Sabbath. But even further, the people agreed to give annually from their resources to preserve and maintain the functions of the temple. Their example demonstrates the generous heart we should also have when it comes to serving others and giving our tithes and offerings to the Lord.

OBSERVATION

Read Nehemiah 10:28–39 from the New International Version or the New King James Version.

New International Version

²⁸ "The rest of the people—priests, Levites, gatekeepers, musicians, temple servants and all who separated themselves from the neighboring

peoples for the sake of the Law of God, together with their wives and all their sons and daughters who are able to understand— [29] all these now join their fellow Israelites the nobles, and bind themselves with a curse and an oath to follow the Law of God given through Moses the servant of God and to obey carefully all the commands, regulations and decrees of the LORD our Lord.

[30] "We promise not to give our daughters in marriage to the peoples around us or take their daughters for our sons.

[31] "When the neighboring peoples bring merchandise or grain to sell on the Sabbath, we will not buy from them on the Sabbath or on any holy day. Every seventh year we will forgo working the land and will cancel all debts.

[32] "We assume the responsibility for carrying out the commands to give a third of a shekel each year for the service of the house of our God: [33] for the bread set out on the table; for the regular grain offerings and burnt offerings; for the offerings on the Sabbaths, at the New Moon feasts and at the appointed festivals; for the holy offerings; for sin offerings to make atonement for Israel; and for all the duties of the house of our God.

[34] "We—the priests, the Levites and the people—have cast lots to determine when each of our families is to bring to the house of our God at set times each year a contribution of wood to burn on the altar of the LORD our God, as it is written in the Law.

[35] "We also assume responsibility for bringing to the house of the LORD each year the firstfruits of our crops and of every fruit tree.

[36] "As it is also written in the Law, we will bring the firstborn of our sons and of our cattle, of our herds and of our flocks to the house of our God, to the priests ministering there.

[37] "Moreover, we will bring to the storerooms of the house of our God, to the priests, the first of our ground meal, of our grain offerings, of the fruit of all our trees and of our new wine and olive oil. And we will bring a tithe of our crops to the Levites, for it is the Levites who collect the tithes in all the towns where we work. [38] A priest descended from

Aaron is to accompany the Levites when they receive the tithes, and the Levites are to bring a tenth of the tithes up to the house of our God, to the storerooms of the treasury. ³⁹ The people of Israel, including the Levites, are to bring their contributions of grain, new wine and olive oil to the storerooms, where the articles for the sanctuary and for the ministering priests, the gatekeepers and the musicians are also kept.

"We will not neglect the house of our God."

NEW KING JAMES VERSION

²⁸ Now the rest of the people—the priests, the Levites, the gatekeepers, the singers, the Nethinim, and all those who had separated themselves from the peoples of the lands to the Law of God, their wives, their sons, and their daughters, everyone who had knowledge and understanding— ²⁹ these joined with their brethren, their nobles, and entered into a curse and an oath to walk in God's Law, which was given by Moses the servant of God, and to observe and do all the commandments of the LORD our Lord, and His ordinances and His statutes: ³⁰ We would not give our daughters as wives to the peoples of the land, nor take their daughters for our sons; ³¹ if the peoples of the land brought wares or any grain to sell on the Sabbath day, we would not buy it from them on the Sabbath, or on a holy day; and we would forego the seventh year's produce and the exacting of every debt.

³² Also we made ordinances for ourselves, to exact from ourselves yearly one-third of a shekel for the service of the house of our God: ³³ for the showbread, for the regular grain offering, for the regular burnt offering of the Sabbaths, the New Moons, and the set feasts; for the holy things, for the sin offerings to make atonement for Israel, and all the work of the house of our God. ³⁴ We cast lots among the priests, the Levites, and the people, for bringing the wood offering into the house of our God, according to our fathers' houses, at the appointed times year by year, to burn on the altar of the LORD our God as it is written in the Law.

³⁵ And we made ordinances to bring the firstfruits of our ground and the firstfruits of all fruit of all trees, year by year, to the house of the

LORD; [36] to bring the firstborn of our sons and our cattle, as it is written in the Law, and the firstborn of our herds and our flocks, to the house of our God, to the priests who minister in the house of our God; [37] to bring the firstfruits of our dough, our offerings, the fruit from all kinds of trees, the new wine and oil, to the priests, to the storerooms of the house of our God; and to bring the tithes of our land to the Levites, for the Levites should receive the tithes in all our farming communities. [38] And the priest, the descendant of Aaron, shall be with the Levites when the Levites receive tithes; and the Levites shall bring up a tenth of the tithes to the house of our God, to the rooms of the storehouse.

[39] For the children of Israel and the children of Levi shall bring the offering of the grain, of the new wine and the oil, to the storerooms where the articles of the sanctuary are, where the priests who minister and the gatekeepers and the singers are; and we will not neglect the house of our God.

EXPLORATION

1. Why was it important for the exiles to review their covenant with God?

_____

_____

_____

_____

2. What areas of life were affected by their agreement with God?

_____

_____

_____

_____

3. In what ways did the people plan to show their devotion to God?

_____

_____

_____

4. What did the people promise to provide "for service of the house of our God" (verse 32)?

_____

_____

_____

5. Why did God desire the people to be generous and give the first of their resources?

_____

_____

_____

6. What does giving back a portion of your resources to God's work say about your priorities?

_____

_____

_____

INSPIRATION

"Whoever compels you to go one mile, go with him two" (Matthew 5:41 NKJV). When Jesus spoke these words, his fellow citizens were living under foreign rule. Roman soldiers imposed high taxes and oppressive laws. This sad state of affairs had existed ever since the Babylonians had destroyed the temple in 586 BC and carried the Judeans into captivity. Though some had returned from geographical exile, the theological and political exile lingered.

First-century Jews were sloshing through a centuries-old morass: oppressed by pagans, looking for the Messiah to deliver them. Some responded by selling out, working the system to their own advantage. Others got out. The writers of the Dead Sea Scrolls at Qumran chose to separate themselves from the wicked world. Still others decided to fight back. The Zealot option was clear: say your prayers, sharpen your sword, and fight a holy war.

Three options: sell out, get out, or fight back.

Jesus introduced a fourth. Serve. Serve the ones who hate you; forgive the ones who hurt you. Take the lowest place, not the highest; seek to serve, not to be served. Retaliate, not in kind but in kindness. He created what we might deem the Society of the Second Mile.

Roman soldiers could legally coerce Jewish citizens into carrying their load for one mile. With nothing more than a command, they could requisition a farmer out of his field or a merchant out of his shop.

In such a case, Jesus said, "Give more than requested." Go two. At the end of one mile, keep going. Surprise the sandals off the soldier by saying, "I haven't done enough for you. I'm going a second mile." Do more than demanded. And do so with joy and grace!

The Society of the Second Mile still exists. Its members surrender Everest-level ambitions so they can help weary climbers find safety. (From *Great Day Every Day* by Max Lucado.)

REACTION

7. In what ways do people still "sell out, get out, or fight back" when dealing with difficulties?

_____

_____

_____

8. Why is it important to "serve the ones who hate you" and "forgive the ones who hurt you"?

_____

_____

_____

_____

_____

_____

9. Why is it important to be generous in sharing the gifts that God has given to you?

_____

_____

_____

_____

_____

_____

10. What do you receive in return when you give money to the church?

_____

_____

_____

_____

_____

_____

11. What is the connection between tithing and worship?

_____

_____

_____

_____

_____

12. What steps can you take to be a steward instead of an owner of your financial resources?

_____

_____

_____

_____

_____

_____

LIFE LESSONS

In the Old Testament, God called his people to support the ministry of the temple and the Levites and priests who served in it. The priests and Levites were not allotted their own land—they survived because of the obedient generosity of God's people. A similar plan is evident in the New Testament. As Paul wrote, "The Lord has commanded that those who preach the gospel should live from the gospel" (1 Corinthians 9:14). Believers were called to give generously to the ministry of its leaders, for "the one who receives instruction in the word should share all good things with their instructor" (Galatians 6:6). When we generously and joyfully give of our resources, we are obedient to God. In fact, we're giving to God. Churches who take good financial care of their pastors and leaders bring joy to the heart of God.

DEVOTION

Father, you deserve the best we can give because all we have comes from you. Forgive us for clinging to our possessions, our time, and our money. Help us to see the importance of giving you the firstfruits of our labors. Teach us what it means to make you the Lord of our lives.

JOURNALING

When are you most tempted to hold back your best from God?

FOR FURTHER READING

To complete the books of Ezra and Nehemiah during this twelve-part study, read Nehemiah 10:28–13:31. For more Bible passages on giving, read Leviticus 27:30–33; Deuteronomy 14:22–28; Proverbs 11:24–26; Malachi 3:8–12; Matthew 6:1–4; 22:15–21; Acts 20:32–35; and 2 Corinthians 9:7–8.

LEADER'S GUIDE FOR SMALL GROUPS

Thank you for your willingness to lead a group through *Life Lessons from Ezra and Nehemiah*. The rewards of being a leader are different from those of participating, and we hope you find your own walk with Jesus deepened by this experience. During the twelve lessons in this study, you will guide your group through selected passages in Ezra and Nehemiah and explore the key themes of the books. There are several elements in this leader's guide that will help you as you structure your study and reflection time, so be sure to follow along and take advantage of each one.

BEFORE YOU BEGIN

Before your first meeting, make sure the group members have their own copy of the *Life Lessons from Ezra and Nehemiah* study guide so they can follow along and have their answers written out ahead of time. Alternately, you can hand out the guides at your first meeting and give the group some time to look over the material and ask any preliminary questions. Be sure to send a sheet around the room during that first meeting and have the members write down their name, phone number, and email address so you can keep in touch with them during the week.

There are several ways to structure the duration of the study. You can choose to cover each lesson individually for a total of twelve weeks of discussion, or you can combine two lessons together per week for a total of six weeks of discussion.

You can also choose to have the group members read just the selected passages of Scripture given in each lesson, or they can cover the entire books of Ezra and Nehemiah by reading the material listed in the "For Further Reading" section at the end of each lesson. The following table illustrates these options:

Twelve-Week Format

Week	Lessons Covered	Simplified Reading	Expanded Reading
1	Following God's Guidance	Ezra 1:1–11	Ezra 1:1–2:70
2	Walking in Faith	Ezra 3:1–11	Ezra 3:1–4:24
3	Celebrating God's Goodness	Ezra 6:13–22	Ezra 5:1–6:22
4	Trusting in God's Protection	Ezra 8:21–32	Ezra 7:1–8:36
5	Dealing with Guilt	Ezra 9:1–15	Ezra 9:1–15
6	True Repentance	Ezra 10:1–17	Ezra 10:1–44
7	Prayer and Action	Nehemiah 1:1–11	Nehemiah 1:1–11
8	Confidence in God	Nehemiah 2:1–20	Nehemiah 2:1–3:16
9	Persevering in Trials	Nehemiah 4:1–23	Nehemiah 3:17–4:23
10	Help for the Hurting	Nehemiah 5:1–13	Nehemiah 5:1–7:73
11	Love and Faithfulness	Nehemiah 9:5–21	Nehemiah 8:1–10:27
12	A Generous Heart	Nehemiah 10:28–39	Nehemiah 10:28–13:31

Six-Week Format

Week	Lessons Covered	Simplified Reading	Expanded Reading
1	Following God's Guidance / Walking in Faith	Ezra 1:1–11; 3:1–11	Ezra 1:1–4:24
2	Celebrating God's Goodness / Trusting in God's Protection	Ezra 6:13–22; 8:21–32	Ezra 5:1–8:36
3	Dealing with Guilt / True Repentance	Ezra 9:1–10:17	Ezra 9:1–10:44
4	Prayer and Action / Confidence in God	Nehemiah 1:1–2:20	Nehemiah 1:1–3:16
5	Persevering in Trials / Help for the Hurting	Nehemiah 4:1–5: 13	Nehemiah 3:17–7:73
6	Love and Faithfulness / A Generous Heart	Nehemiah 9:5–21; 10:28–39	Nehemiah 8:1–13:31

Generally, the ideal size you will want for the group is between eight to ten people, which ensures everyone will have enough time to participate in discussions. If you have more people, you might want to break up the main group into smaller subgroups. Encourage those who show up at the first meeting to commit to attending the duration of the study, as this will help the group members get to know each other, create stability for the group, and help you know how to prepare each week.

Each of the lessons begins with a brief reflection that highlights the theme you will be discussing that week. As you begin your group time, have the group members briefly respond to the opening question to get them thinking about the topic at hand. Some people may want to tell a long story in response to one of these questions, but the goal is to keep the answers brief. Ideally, you want everyone in the group to get a chance to answer, so try to keep the responses to just a few minutes. If you have more talkative group members, say up front that everyone needs to limit his or her answer to two minutes.

Give the group members a chance to answer, but tell them to feel free to pass if they wish. With the rest of the study, it's generally not a good idea to have everyone answer every question—a free-flowing discussion is more desirable. But with the opening reflection question, you can go around the circle. Encourage shy people to share, but don't force them.

Before your first meeting, let the group members know how the lessons are broken down. During your group discussion time the members will be drawing on the answers they wrote to the Exploration and Reaction sections, so encourage them to always complete these ahead of time. Also, invite them to bring any questions and insights they uncovered while reading to your next meeting, especially if they had a breakthrough moment or if they didn't understand something they read.

WEEKLY PREPARATION

As the leader, there are a few things you should do to prepare for each meeting:

- *Read through the lesson.* This will help you to become familiar with the content and know how to structure the discussion times.
- *Decide which questions you want to discuss.* Depending on how you structure your group time, you may not be able to cover every question. So select the questions ahead of time that you absolutely want the group to explore.
- *Be familiar with the questions you want to discuss.* When the group meets you'll be watching the clock, so you want to make sure you are familiar with the Bible study questions you have selected. You can then spend time in the passage again when the group meets. In this way, you'll ensure you have the passage more deeply in your mind than your group members.
- *Pray for your group.* Pray for your group members throughout the week and ask God to lead them as they study his Word.
- *Bring extra supplies to your meeting.* The members should bring their own pens for writing notes, but it's a good idea to have extras available for those who forget. You may also want to bring paper and additional Bibles.

Note that in many cases there will not be one "right" answer to the question. Answers will vary, especially when the group members are being asked to share their personal experiences.

STRUCTURING THE DISCUSSION TIME

You will need to determine with your group how long you want to meet each week so you can plan your time accordingly. Generally, most groups like to meet for either sixty minutes or ninety minutes, so you could use one of the following schedules:

Section	60 Minutes	90 Minutes
WELCOME (members arrive and get settled)	5 minutes	10 minutes
REFLECTION (discuss the opening question for the lesson)	10 minutes	15 minutes
DISCUSSION (discuss the Bible study questions in the Exploration and Reaction sections)	35 minutes	50 minutes
PRAYER/CLOSING (pray together as a group and dismiss)	10 minutes	15 minutes

As the group leader, it is up to you to keep track of the time and keep things moving along according to your schedule. You might want to set a timer for each segment so both you and the group members know when your time is up. (Note that there are some good phone apps for timers that play a gentle chime or other pleasant sound instead of a disruptive noise.) Don't feel pressured to cover every question you have selected if the group has a good discussion going. Again, it's not necessary to go around the circle and make everyone share.

Don't be concerned if the group members are silent or slow to share. People are often quiet when they are pulling together their ideas, and this might be a new experience for them. Just ask a question and let it hang in the air until someone shares. You can then say, "Thank you. What about others? What came to you when you reflected on the passage?"

GROUP DYNAMICS

Leading a group through *Life Lessons from Ezra and Nehemiah* will prove to be highly rewarding both to you and your group members—but that doesn't mean you will not encounter any challenges along the way! Discussions can get off track. Group members may not be sensitive to the needs and ideas of others. Some might worry they will be expected to talk about matters that make them feel awkward. Others may express comments that result in disagreements. To help ease this strain on you and the group, consider the following ground rules:

- When someone raises a question or comment that is off the main topic, suggest you deal with it another time, or, if you feel led to go in that direction, let the group know you will be spending some time discussing it.
- If someone asks a question you don't know how to answer, admit it and move on. At your discretion, feel free to invite group members to comment on questions that call for personal experience.
- If you find one or two people are dominating the discussion time, direct a few questions to others in the group. Outside the main group time, ask the more dominating members to help you draw out the quieter ones. Work to make them a part of the solution instead of the problem.
- When a disagreement occurs, encourage the group members to process the matter in love. Encourage those on opposite sides to restate what they heard the other side say about the matter, and then invite each side to evaluate if that perception is accurate. Lead the group in examining other Scriptures related to the topic and look for common ground.

When any of these issues arise, encourage your group members to follow the words from the Bible: "Love one another" (John 13:34), "If it is possible, as far as it depends on you, live at peace with everyone" (Romans 12:18), and, "Be quick to listen, slow to speak and slow to become angry" (James 1:19).

Thank you again for taking the time to lead your group. May God reward your efforts and dedication and make your time together in this study fruitful for his kingdom.

ALSO AVAILABLE IN THE
LIFE LESSONS SERIES

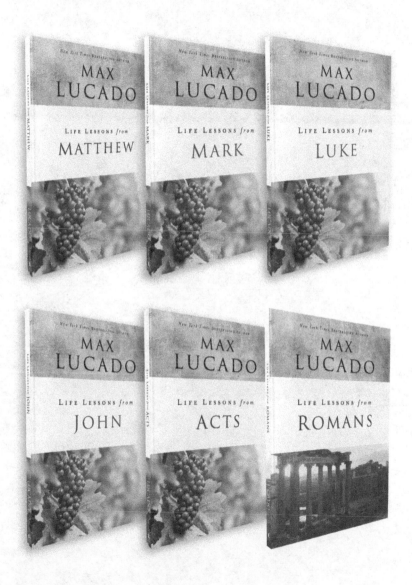

*Now available wherever books
and ebooks are sold.*